U0331439

普通高等学校网络工程专业规划教材

计算机网络英语

陈伟宏 黄雪华 吴宏斌 编著

清华大学出版社

北京

内 容 简 介

本书是以中英双语形式编写的计算机网络教材。全书分为计算机网络概述、物理层、数据链路层、网络层、传输层、应用层、网络安全、网络新技术和计算机网络英语翻译技巧九个单元，每个单元的内容包括课文、语法注释、词汇短语、计算机专业术语、练习、扩展阅读和参考译文，以帮助读者理解和掌握课文内容。书后附有部分习题答案。

本书可作为计算机及相关专业大学本、专科生的专业英语教材，也可作为计算机网络工程及相关专业的计算机网络的辅助教材。同时，对于想了解计算机网络知识的网络用户，也不失为一本较好的网络英语读物。

图书在版编目（CIP）数据

计算机网络英语/陈伟宏，黄雪华，吴宏斌编著. —北京：清华大学出版社，2014（2024.1 重印）
（普通高等学校网络工程专业规划教材）
ISBN 978-7-302-35546-5

Ⅰ. ①计…　Ⅱ. ①陈…　②黄…　③吴…　Ⅲ. ①计算机网络－英语－高等学校－教材　Ⅳ. ①H31

中国版本图书馆 CIP 数据核字（2014）第 034913 号

责任编辑：沈　洁　李　晔
封面设计：常雪影
责任校对：白　蕾
责任印制：宋　林

出版发行：清华大学出版社
　　　网　　　址：https://www.tup.com.cn，https://www.wqxuetang.com
　　　地　　　址：北京清华大学学研大厦 A 座　　　　　邮　　　编：100084
　　　社 总 机：010-83470000　　　　　　　　　　　邮　　　购：010-62786544
　　　投稿与读者服务：010-62776969，c-service@tup.tsinghua.edu.cn
　　　质量反馈：010-62772015，zhiliang@tup.tsinghua.edu.cn
　　　课件下载：https://www.tup.com.cn，010-83470236
印 装 者：三河市龙大印装有限公司
经　　　销：全国新华书店
开　　　本：185mm×260mm　　　印　张：11.5　　　　　字　　　数：279 千字
版　　　次：2014 年 5 月第 1 版　　　　　　　　　　　印　　　次：2024 年 1 月第 10 次印刷
定　　　价：29.00 元

产品编号：057918-02

FOREWORD

前　言

随着社会信息化,计算机网络在人们的工作和生活中已经普及,并正改变着人类的生活方式。了解计算机网络已经成为现代人必备的基本技能之一。众所周知,计算机网络源于美国,其原理与应用开发技术大多以英文撰写,大多数计算机网络方面的最新研究成果都以英文公布于众。因此,不管是计算机及相关专业工程技术人员、从事计算机科学与技术的教学科研人员,还是一般的计算机网络用户,掌握一定的计算机网络英语基础知识具有重要意义。

本书是以英语形式介绍计算机网络原理,为开设计算机网络英语课程而编写的 21 世纪教材。全书分为计算机网络概述、物理层、数据链路层、网络层、传输层、应用层、网络安全、网络新技术和计算机网络英语翻译技巧共九个单元,为广大读者提供了计算机网络领域的基本原理及最新技术。第一单元是计算机网络概述,主要介绍计算机网络的概念、发展、应用、分类及 OSI 参考模型、TCP/IP 协议。第二单元是物理层,主要介绍数据通信原理、传输介质、电路交换和分组交换技术。第三单元是数据链路层,主要讲述差错检测与纠正,详细介绍了海明码和纠错码;举例说明数据链路协议 HDLC、PPP;介绍了以太网和无线局域网、CSMA/CD、曼切斯特编码、CSMA/CA;介绍了网络互连设备、集线器、路由器、网桥。第四单元是网络层,介绍了路由算法,包括最短路径路由算法、洪泛算法、Bellman-Ford 路由算法、链路状态路由算法;讲述了 IPv4 协议、子网、CIDR、NAT;介绍了 Internet 中的控制协议及路由,包括 ICMP、ARP、RARP、RIP、OSPF、BGP;讲述了 IPv6 协议及 IPv4 到 IPv6 的过渡。第五单元是传输层,介绍了传输服务、用户数据报协议 UDP、传输控制协议 TCP 及其拥塞控制。第六单元是应用层,介绍了 WWW、FTP、HTTP、E-mail、DNS 以及网络仿真软件 OMNeT++、网络编程语言 Java。第七单元是网络安全,介绍了密码学基础、对称密钥算法、公开密钥算法。第八单元是网络新技术,介绍物联网和云计算。第九单元是计算机网络英语翻译技巧,介绍了计算机网络英语的翻译原则,计算机网络英语的构词法、专业术语、计算机网络英语中的常用语法,包括动词不定式、动名词、分词、被动语态、定语从句等在翻译时的技巧。

本书每个单元的内容包括课文、语法注释、词汇短语(对课文中的重要词语

I

FOREWORD

给出了音标、词性和译文)、计算机专业术语、练习、扩展阅读、参考译文。为了更好地表达专业原理，书中配有很多插图和说明，帮助广大读者既掌握计算机网络基本原理又提高计算机网络专业英语阅读水平。

本书由陈伟宏、黄雪华、吴宏斌编著。

由于计算机网络快速发展，新知识、新名词层出不穷，书中有些词汇尚无规范译法，加上作者水平有限，难免有欠缺之处，恳请广大读者批评指正，我们的联系方式为 107531852@qq.com。

编者

2014 年 2 月

CONTENTS

目　录

C O N T E N T S

CONTENTS

CONTENTS

CONTENTS

C O N T E N T S

Unit 1　Computer Network Basics

Section A　Introduction to Computer Networks

I. Introduction

Today, networks are everywhere and network technologies are evolving rapidly. Just when you think you have **broadband** access network under control, along comes **WiFi** and the **mobile network**. ① Just as you get comfortable with your campus-wide network, mobile Internet using wireless connection appeared that can be used by anyone at anytime and anywhere.

II. What's the Computer Network?

The computer network is such a network consisting of two or more computers that are linked in order to share resources, exchange files, or allow **electronic communications**. The computers on a network may be linked through **cables**, telephone lines, **radio waves**, **satellites** and so on. Resource sharing and data communication are the main function of computer networks. The Internet is not a single network but a network of networks and the World Wide Web is a **distributed** system that runs on top of the Internet.

III. Evolution of Computer Networks

The first computer network emerged in 1969, namely **ARPANET**. ② With the increasing of the number of the networks, machines and users connected to the ARPANET grew rapidly and **TCP/IP** gradually became the only official **protocol** and Internet **was born** in 1983 in result. They[③] have **inherited** many useful properties from older and more widely adopted telephone networks. This is not surprising, since both computers and telephones are **universal instruments** of communications.

The basic architecture of the Internet mainly **goes through** three stages. But the time is **overlapped** for their existence and they don't separate from each other completely. The first stage is such a process from a network ARPANET to the interconnection network. The **architecture** of the ARPANET is **split into** two parts: **subnet** and **host.** The subnet part consists of the **IMP** end of the host-IMP connection, the IMP-IMP protocol, and a source IMP to destination IMP protocol designed to improve reliability. The original ARPANET design is shown in Figure 1.1.

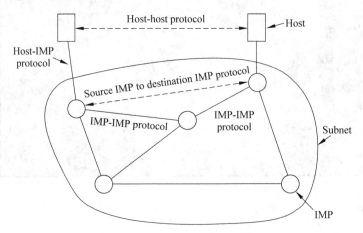

Figure 1.1   The original ARPANET design

The feature of the second stage is the three-level architecture used in the Internet. **NSF** (the U. S. National Science Foundation) funded some regional networks that connected to the **backbone** to allow users at thousands of universities, research labs, libraries, and museums to access any of the **supercomputers** and to communicate with one another. The complete network, including the backbone and the regional networks, was called NSFNET.

The feature of the third stage is the multi-level **ISP** architecture used in the Internet. The **glue** that holds the Internet together is the **TCP/IP reference model** and **TCP/IP protocol stack**. TCP/IP makes universal service possible. What does it actually mean to be on the Internet? Our definition is that a machine is on the Internet if it runs the TCP/IP protocol stack, has an IP address, and can send IP packets to all the other machines on the Internet.

Although the **topology** of the Internet is very complicated, its architecture can be split into two parts according to the working mechanism: **communication subnet** and **resource subnet.** The resource subnet is composed of all hosts connected to the Internet, and the communication subnet consists of a large number of networks and **routers** connecting such networks.

IV. Applications of Computer Networks

It is worth devoting some time to point out applications of computer networks. ① We will start with traditional uses at companies and for individuals and then move on to recent developments regarding mobile users and home networking.

1. Business Applications

Many companies have a **substantial** number of computers that are connected to share resources. However, probably even more important than sharing **physical** resources such as printers, scanners, is sharing information. The client-server model and the **peer-to-peer** model are widely used and form the basis of much network usage. They are applicable when the client and server are both in the same building or far apart.

Except for information, computer networks can provide a powerful communication medium among employees, such as E-mail. Another form of computer-assisted communication is **videoconferencing.** Using this technology, employees at distant locations can hold a meeting, seeing and hearing each other and even writing on a shared virtual blackboard. Videoconferencing is a powerful tool for eliminating the cost and time previously devoted to travel. **E-commerce** is also one of the important business applications. Many companies provide catalogs of their goods and services online and take orders on-line. It is called e-commerce.

2. Home Applications

Why do people buy computers for home use? Initially, for word processing and games, but in recent years it is for Internet access. Some of the more popular uses of the Internet for home users are as follows:

- Access to remote information.
- Person-to-person communication.
- Interactive entertainment.
- Electronic commerce.

3. Mobile Users

Mobile computers, such as notebook computers and personal **digital assistants** (PDAs), are one of the fastest-growing segments of the computer industry. Since having a wired connection is impossible in cars and airplanes, there is a lot of interest in wireless networks. For the portable office, people on the road often want to use their portable electronic equipment to send and receive messages, electronic mail, surf the Web, access remote files, and log on to remote machines.

4. Social Issues

Along with the good comes the bad. ⑤ The widespread introduction of networking has introduced new social, **ethical**, and political problems. The Internet makes it possible to find information quickly, but a lot of it is ill-informed, misleading, or downright wrong. Computer networks have also introduced new kinds of antisocial and criminal behavior. **Electronic junk mail** (spam) has become a part of life because some people have collected millions of e-mail addresses and sell them on CD-ROMs to **would-be** marketers[⑥]. E-mail messages containing active content can contain viruses that **wreak havoc**. A lot of these problems could be solved if the technology of the computer security is well established.

V. Classification of Computer Networks

Computer networks can be classified based on several factors, such as the scale, transmission technology, topologies and network users. The most known classification is based on the physical size of the network, as shown in Figure 1.2. At the top are the personal area networks that are for one person. Beyond the personal area networks are come longer range networks. These can be divided into local, metropolitan and wide area networks. At the same time, the connection of two or more networks is called an **internetwork**. The worldwide Internet is a well-known example of an internet.

Interprocessor distance	Processors located in same	Example
1m	Square meter	Personal area network
10m	Room	
100m	Building	Local area network
1km	Campus	
10km	City	Metropolitan area network
100km	Country	
1000km	Continent	Wide area network
10 000km	Planet	The Internet

Figure 1.2   Classification of networks by scale

Local area networks, generally called **LANs**, are privately-owned networks within a single building or campus of up to a few kilometers in size. A metropolitan area network, or **MAN**, covers a city. The best-known example of a MAN is the cable television network available in many cities. A wide area network, or **WAN**, spans a large **geographical** area, often a country or continent. It contains communication subnet and resource subnet.

Network topology is the arrangement or mapping of the elements of a network. The basic types of topologies are: **Bus**, **Star**, **Ring**, **Tree** and **Hybrid**. They are shown in Figure 1.3.

According to the transmission technology, there are two types in widespread use: **broadcast** links and **point-to-point** links. Broadcast networks have a single communication

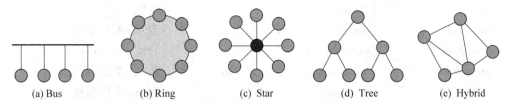

Figure 1.3　Classification of networks by topology

channel that is shared by all the machines on the network. Short messages sent by any machine are received by all the others. This mode of operation is called broadcasting. Some broadcast systems also support transmission to a subset of the machines, something known as **multicasting**. In contrast, point-to-point networks consist of many connections between individual pairs of machines. Point-to-point transmission with one sender and one receiver is sometimes called **unicasting**.

Notes

① Just when you think you have broadband access network under control, along comes WiFi and the mobile network. 在这里 have sth. under control 是指"掌握什么事情，熟悉什么事情"，而后半句用了倒装，主语是 WiFi and the mobile network，这里用倒装主要是用来强调网络技术更新快。当你才掌握宽带接入，无线和移动网络就出现了。

② ARPANET：所谓"阿帕"，是美国高级研究计划署（ARPA, Advanced Research Project Agency）的简称。其核心机构之一是信息处理处（IPTO, Information Processing Techniques Office），一直在关注计算机图形、网络通信、超级计算机等研究课题，阿帕网为美国国防部高级研究计划署开发的世界上第一个运营的封包交换网络，它是全球互联网的始祖。

③ They have inherited many useful properties from older and more widely adopted telephone networks. 这里的 they 指代的是前面的 Internet 和 ARPANET，表示因特网和阿帕网都继承了电话网有用的性质。

④ It is worth devoting some time to point out applications of computer networks. 这里 be worth doing sth. 是指"值得花时间或精力去做什么事情"，be worth 后面接动词的-ing 形式。

⑤ Along with the good comes the bad. 这一句也用了倒装，类似第①条注释，这里的倒装用来强调"坏的跟随好的同时出现"。

⑥ Electronic junk mail (spam) has become a part of life because people have collected millions of e-mail addresses and sell them on CD-ROMs to would-be marketers. 这句话采用了现在完成时态，spam 也指垃圾邮件的意思，sell sth. on sth. 表示"以什么形式出售"，这里的 would-be 是个形容词，表示"自称的"。

New Words and Phrases

| access | ['ækses] | *n.* | 进入；接入 |

cable	['keibl]	n.	电缆
satellite	['sætəlait]	n.	卫星;人造卫星
distribute	[di'stribju:t]	vt.	分配;散布;分布
protocol	['prəutəkɔl]	n.	协议;草案;礼仪
inherit	[in'herit]	vt.	继承;遗传而得
universal	['ju:ni'vɜ:sl]	adj.	普遍的;通用的;全体的
instrument	['instrəmənt]	n.	仪器;工具;乐器;器械
adopt	[ə'dɔpt]	vt.	采取;接受;收养
architecture	['ɑ:ki'tektʃə]	n.	建筑学;体系结构;架构
go through			参加;经受
overlap	['ovə'læp]	vt.	与…重叠;与…同时发生
split into			分成
destination	[ˌdesti'neiʃən]	n.	目的地,终点
original	[ə'ridʒənl]	adj.	原始的;最初的;独创的
glue	[glu:]	n.	胶水;胶粘物;粘聚力
substantial	[səb'stænʃl]	adj.	大量的;实质的
scanner	['skænə]	n.	扫描仪;扫描器
catalog	['kætələ:g]	n.	目录;登记
take order			点酒水、点菜;服从指挥
online	[ˌɔn'lain]	n.	在线;联机
medium	['mi:diəm]	n.	方法;媒体;媒介
entertainment	[ˌentə'teinmənt]	n.	娱乐;消遣;款待
mobile	[məu'bail]	adj.	移动的;易变的;非固定的
segment	['segmənt]	n.	段;部分
equipment	[i'kwipmənt]	n.	设备,装备;器材
log on			登录;注册
issue	['iʃu:]	n.	问题;流出;期号;发行物
ethical	['eθikl]	adj.	伦理的;道德的
ill-formed	[il'fɔ:md]	adj.	不合语法的;不规范的
misleading	[ˌmis'li:diŋ]	adj.	令人误解的;引入歧途的
marketer	['mɑ:kitə]	n.	市场商人;市场营销人员
would-be	['wudbi:]	adj.	想要成为的;自称的
wreak	[ri:k]	vt.	发泄;报仇
havoc	['hævək]	n.	大破坏;蹂躏
wreak havoc			肆虐;造成严重破坏
virus	['vairəs]	n.	病毒;恶毒;毒害
establish	[i'stæbliʃ]	vt.	建立;创办;安置
classify	['klæsifai]	vt.	分类;分等
transmission	[træns'miʃən]	n.	传递;传送;播送

topology	[təˈpɔlədʒi]	*n.*	拓扑学
physical	[ˈfizikəl]	*adj.*	物理的；物质的
metropolitan	[ˌmetrəˈpɔlitən]	*adj.*	大都市的
span	[spæn]	*vt.*	跨越；持续；以手指测量
geographical	[ˌdʒiːəˈgræfikl]	*adj.*	地理的；地理学的
channel	[ˈtʃænl]	*n.*	通道；频道；海峡

Computer Terminologies

computer network	计算机网络
broadband	宽带
WiFi(Wireless Fidelity)	无线保真
Mobile Internet	移动互联网
electronic communication	电子通信
radio wave	无线电波
World Wide Web	万维网
Internet	因特网
TCP/IP(Transmission Control Protocol/Internet Protocol)	传输控制协议/网际协议
IMP (Interface Message Processor)	接口信息处理器
subnet	子网
host	主机
reliability	可靠性
NSF(National Science Foundation)	(美国)国家科学基金会
backbone	骨干网
supercomputer	巨型机
regional network	区域网
ISP(Internet Service Provider)	因特网服务提供者
TCP/IP reference model	TCP/IP 参考模型
TCP/IP protocol stack	TCP/IP 协议栈
IP (Internet Protocol)	互联网协议
packet	数据包
communication subnet	通信子网
resource subnet	资源子网
router	路由器
client-server	客户-服务器
peer-to-peer	对等网络
videoconferencing	视频会议
electronic-commerce	电子商务
PDA(Personal Digital Assistant)	个人数字助理
portable office	移动办公

surf the web	在网上冲浪
electronic junk mail(spam)	电子垃圾邮件
Internetwork	互联网络
LAN(local area network)	局域网
MAN(Metropolitan Area Network)	城域网
WAN(Wide Area Network)	广域网
bus	总线
star	星型
ring	环型
tree	树型
hybrid	混合型
broadcasting	广播
point-to-point	点对点
multicasting	组播
unicasting	单播

Exercises

I. Translate these English sentences into Chinese.

1. Just as you get comfortable with your campus-wide network, mobile Internet using wireless connection appeared that can be used by anyone at anytime and anywhere.

2. The computer network is such a network consisting of two or more computers that are linked in order to share resources, exchange files, or allow electronic communications.

3. The computers on a network may be linked through cables, telephone lines, radio waves, satellites and so on.

4. The basic architecture of the Internet mainly goes through three stages.

5. NSF (the U. S. National Science Foundation) funded some regional networks that connected to the backbone to allow users at thousands of universities, research labs, libraries, and museums to access any of the supercomputers and to communicate with one another.

6. The glue that holds the Internet together is the TCP/IP reference model and TCP/IP protocol stack.

7. Our definition is that a machine is on the Internet if it runs the TCP/IP protocol stack, has an IP address, and can send IP packets to all the other machines on the Internet.

8. For the portable office, people on the road often want to use their portable electronic equipment to send and receive messages, electronic mail, surf the Web, access remote files, and log on to remote machines.

II. Answer the questions

1. Tell the differences between LAN，MAN，WAN and PAN.
2. Describe the classification of the computer network.
3. What is the computer network composed of?
4. Tell the history of the computer network.

Extending Your Reading

An interview with Leonard Kleinrock

Leonard Kleinrock is a professor of computer science of the University of Califonia，Los Angeles. In 1969，his computer at UCIA became the first node of the Internet. His creation of packet-switching principles in 1961 became the technology behind the Internet. Leonard is also the chairman and founder of Nomadix，Inc.，a company whose technology provides greater accessibility of broadband Internet service. He received his B. E. E. from the City College of New York(CCNY) and his masters and PhD in electrical engineering from MIT.

参考译文

计算机网络概述

如今,计算机网络无处不在,网络技术迅猛发展。当你刚掌握了宽带接入网络,无线和移动网络便随之而来。当你还在悠然自在地使用校园网时,任何人在任何时候、任何地点都能无线接入的移动网络出现了。

什么是计算机网络?

计算机网络是由两台或者多台计算机相互连接形成的网络,以共享资源、交换文件以及电子通信为目的。网络中的计算机可以通过电缆、电话线、无线电波、卫星等连接。计算机网络的主要功能是资源共享和数据通信。因特网不是单一的网络,而是网络中的网络,而万维网是运行在因特网之上的一个分布式系统。

计算机网络的发展

第一个计算机网络出现在 1969 年,叫阿帕网。随着接入阿帕网的机器和用户数量快速增长,TCP/IP(传输控制协议/网际协议)逐渐成了唯一的官方通信协议,因特网最终产生于1983 年。

它们从更为古老和使用广泛的电话网上继承了很多有意义的性质。这一点并不奇怪,因为计算机和电话都是使用广泛的通信设备。

因特网的基本体系结构主要经历了三个阶段。但是这三个阶段的时间是重叠的,并不能完全分隔开。第一个阶段是从阿帕网到网络互连的一个过程。阿帕网分成两个部分:子网和主机。子网部分由主机与 IMP 连接之中的 IMP(接口信息处理器)端、IMP 间协议,以及用来提高可靠性的源 IMP 到目的 IMP 之间的协议构成。最初的阿帕网设计如图 1.1 所示。

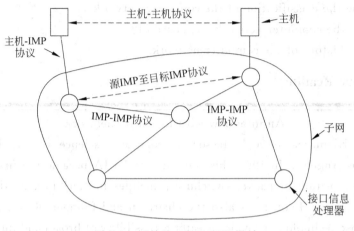

图 1.1　原始的 ARPANET 设计

第二个阶段的特点是因特网中的三层结构。NSF(美国国家科学基金会)资助了一些连接到骨干网的区域网络,这些网络允许成千上万的大学、研究实验室、图书馆、博物馆这些用户接入巨型主机实现互连。包含主干网和区域网的整个完整的网络叫做国家科学基金网。

第三个阶段的特点是因特网中采用了多级 Internet 服务提供商的结构。TCP/IP 参考模型和 TCP/IP 协议栈把整个因特网粘合在一起。TCP/IP 协议使得一切的服务成为可能。接入因特网到底指什么意思呢? 一台机器接入因特网的定义是:它运行 TCP/IP 协议栈,有 IP 地址并且能发送 IP 包到因特网上的其他机器。

虽然因特网的拓扑非常复杂,但是它的结构可以根据其工作方式分成两部分:通信子网和资源子网。资源子网由连接到因特网上所有的主机组成,通信子网由大量网络和连接这些网络的路由器组成。

计算机网络应用

下面值得花时间来谈谈计算机网络的应用。首先介绍传统的公司及个人网络使用,再介绍移动网络用户以及家庭网络。

商业应用

许多公司都有相当数量的计算机相互连接共享资源。然而,比起共享打印机、扫描仪这样的硬件资源,共享信息更为重要。客户服务器模型和对等网络模型是广泛使用的模型且是形成许多网络的基础。客户机和服务器无论是在一栋建筑内还是相距很远,它们都是可行的。

除了共享信息以外,计算机网络还可以在员工之间提供一个强有力的交流媒介,如电子邮件。视频会议是计算机辅助交流的另外一种方式。利用视频会议,员工在相距很远的地方都可以举行会议,能相互看见和听见,甚至还可以在一个共享的虚拟的黑板上写字。视频会议是一个强有力的工具,它可以减少因为旅行所带来的时间和资金成本。电子商务也是商业应用中的一种重要的方式。很多公司在线提供了其产品目录、服务以及订购功能。

家庭应用

为什么人们为了家庭应用而购买计算机呢？起初是用来处理文字、玩游戏，然而近来主要是用来接入因特网。一些比较流行的家庭网络应用如下：

- 获取远程信息。
- 个人通信。
- 互动娱乐。
- 电子商务。

移动用户

移动计算机，如笔记本以及个人数字助理是计算机产业中发展最快速的部分之一。因为在小车和飞机上不可能进行有线接入，于是无线网络引起了广泛的关注。为了可以移动办公，人们在途中经常想要使用便携的电子设备进行发送、接收信息和邮件、浏览网页、获取远程文件以及登录远程机器。

社会问题

往往祸福相依。网络的广泛使用引入了新的社会、伦理、政治问题。因特网使得我们可以快速地找到信息，但很多的信息是不完整的、误导人的其至完全错误的。计算机网络还导致了新的反社会和犯罪行为。由于一些人收集了成千上万的邮件地址并以光盘的形式卖给自称为商人的人，因此垃圾邮件也成了生活的一部分。电子邮件信息包含的活动内容里面可能含有很多在网上肆虐的病毒。如果计算机安全技术成熟，许多这样的问题都能解决。

计算机网络分类

计算机网络可以基于几类因素进行分类，如网络规模、传输技术、拓扑以及网络用户。最出名的分类方法是基于网络的物理范围，如图1.2所示。在图片的最上面部分是个人区域网。除了个人区域网络外，其他都是较长距离的网络了。它可以被分为局域网、城域网和广域网。同时，两个或两个以上的网络连接叫网络互连。国际因特网是一个著名的网络互连的例子。

处理器之间距离	处理器所在位置	例子
1m	一平方米范围	个人区域网
10m	同一房间	局域网
100m	同一建筑物	局域网
1km	同一校园	局域网
10km	同一城市	城域网
100km	同一国家	广域网
1000km	同一个洲	广域网
10 000km	同一行星	Internet

图 1.2　网络按照规模分类

局域网络,简称 LAN,范围大约在几公里内的私有网络,位于一栋建筑或者一个校园内。城域网简称 MAN,它的范围覆盖了一个城市。最著名的城域网例子就是现在很多城市都在用的有限电视网络。广域网简称 WAN,它跨越一个很大的地理区域,通常是一个国家或者大陆。它包含通信子网和资源子网。

网络拓扑是网络中元素的布局或者映射。基本的拓扑类型有总线型、星型、环型、树型以及混合型,如图 1.3 所示。

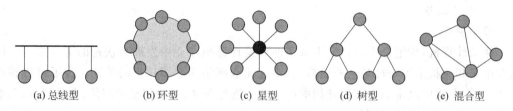

(a) 总线型   (b) 环型   (c) 星型   (d) 树型   (e) 混合型

图 1.3　网络拓扑分类

根据传输技术分类,广泛使用的两种类型:广播链路和点对点链路。在广播网络中所有机器共享一条单一通信通道。任一台机器发出信息,其他所有机器接收信息。这种工作模式叫做广播。一些广播系统也支持组播,信息传输给部分机器。与此相反,点对点网络则是由许多连接构成,由每一个连接对应一对机器。一台机器发送一台机器接收的点对点传输,有时被称为单播。

Section B　Reference Models

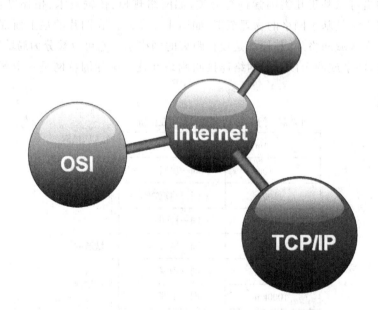

I. Introduction

When computers or other **terminal** equipments exchange data, the **procedures** involved are quite complex.[①] It is clear that there must be a high degree of cooperation between two computer networks. To reduce their design **complexity**, the tasks is **broken up into** subtasks, each of which is implemented separately. Most networks are organized as a **stack** of layers or levels, and each one is built upon the one below it, as shown in Figure 1.4. The number of layers, the name of each layer, the contents of each layer, and the function of each layer differ from network to network. Each layer offer certain service to the higher layer. In a sense, each layer is a kind of virtual machine. Between each pair of **adjacent** layers is an interface, by which the layer offers services to the layer above.

Of course, it takes two to communication. The entities comprising the **corresponding** layers on different machines are called **peers**. [2] A protocol is an **agreement** between the communicating peers on how communication is to proceed. The key features of a protocol are as follows.

- **Syntax**: Concerns the format of the data blocks.
- **Semantics**: Including control information for coordination and error handling.
- **Timing**: Includes speed matching and sequencing.

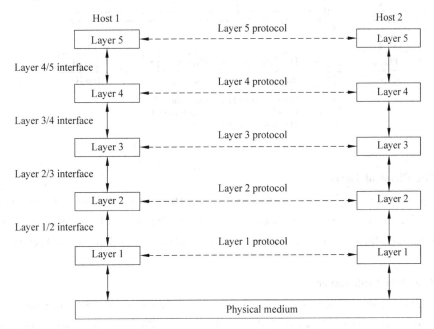

Figure 1.4　Layers, protocols and interfaces

In general, a set of layers and protocols is called the network architecture. Two important network architectures, the OSI reference model and the TCP/IP protocol suite, have served as the standardized framework.

II. The OSI Reference Model

The **OSI model** is based on a **proposal** developed by the International Standards Organization (ISO). It is called the **ISO** OSI (Open Systems Interconnection) Reference Model because it deals with connecting open systems—that is, systems that are open for communication with other systems. We call it the OSI model for short.

The OSI model has seven layers, as shown in Figure 1.5. We will discuss each layer of the model in turn, starting at the bottom layer.

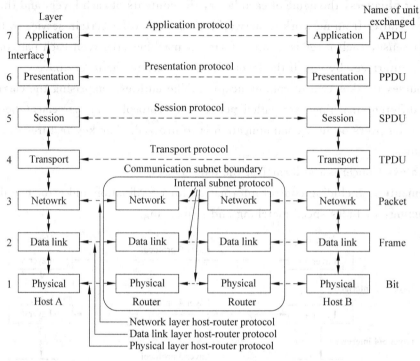

Figure1.5　The OSI reference model

1. The Physical Layer

The physical layer is concerned with transmitting raw bits over the communication channel. The design issues here deal with the **mechanical**, **electrical**, functional, and procedural characteristics to access the physical medium, which lies below the physical layer.

2. The Data Link Layer

The main task of the data link layer is to provide for the reliable transfer of information across the physical link, including sending frames with the necessary **synchronization**, error control and flow control. The processing unit in the data link layer is the frame.

3. The Network Layer

The network layer controls the operation of the subnet and is the lowest layer that deals with end-to-end transmission. The processing unit of the network layer is the packet and its main functions are routing selection, **congestion** control and internetworking. One of key design issues is determining how packets are routed from source to destination. To achieve its goals, the network layer must know about the topology of the communication subnet and choose appropriate paths through it with load balancing.

4. The Transport Layer

The basic function of the transport layer is to accept data from above, split it up into the smaller units if need be, pass these to the network layer, and ensure that the pieces all arrive correctly at the other end. Furthermore, all this must be done efficiently and in a way that isolates the upper layers from the inevitable changes in the hardware technology. The transport layer is a true end-to-end layer, all the way from the source to the destination.

5. The Session Layer

The **session layer** allows users on different machines to establish sessions between them. It offers various services, including dialog control, **token** management, and synchronization.

6. The Presentation Layer

The **presentation layer** is concerned with the syntax and semantics of the information transmitted. It manages the abstract data structures and allows higher-level data structures to be defined and exchanged.

7. The Application Layer

The application layer contains a variety of protocols that are commonly needed by users. One widely-used application protocol is **HTTP** (Hyper Text Transfer Protocol), which is the basis for the World Wide Web. In addition, **general-purpose** applications such as file transfer, E-mail, multimedia are considered residing at this layer.

III. The TCP/IP Reference Model

The TCP/IP architecture is a result of protocol research and development conducted on the experimental packet-switched network, ARPANET. It is generally referred to as the TCP/IP protocol suite. The TCP/IP model organizes the communication task into four independent layers: **the host-to-network layer, the Internet layer, the transport layer, the application layer.**

The lowest layer in the TCP/IP reference model is the host-to-network layer. It does not really say much about what happens here, except to point out that the host has to connect to the network using some protocol. This protocol is not defined and varies from host to host and network to network.

The second layer from bottom to up is the internet layer. It defines an official packet format and protocol called IP (Internet Protocol). Its function is to deliver IP packets where they are supposed to go and packet routing is the major issue here. The TCP/IP internet layer is similar in functionality to the OSI network layer.

The layer above the internet layer in the TCP/IP model is the transport layer. It is designed to allow peer entities on the source and destination hosts to carry on a conversation, just as in the OSI transport layer.

The TCP/IP model does not have session or presentation layers. On top of the transport layer is the application layer. It contains all the higher-level protocols, such as **TELNET, FTP, SMTP**, HTTP and so on. The OSI and TCP/IP reference models are shown in Figure 1.6.

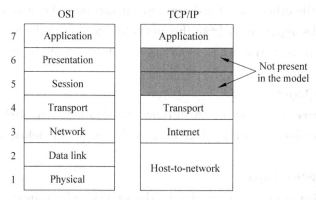

Figure 1.6   The OSI and TCP/IP reference models

IV. A Comparison of the OSI and TCP/IP Reference Models

The OSI and TCP/IP reference models have much in common. Both are based on the concept of a stack of independent protocols. Also, the functionality of the layers is roughly similar.

Despite these fundamental similarities, the two models still have many differences.

(1) Three concepts are central to the OSI model: services, interfaces and protocols. But the TCP/IP model did not originally clearly distinguish between service, interface, and protocol. Probably the biggest contribution of the OSI model is to make the distinction between these three concepts explicit.

(2) Different numbers of layers. The OSI model has seven layers and the TCP/IP has four layers. Both have (inter)network, transport, and application layers, but other layers are different.

(3) The Third difference is in the area of **connectionless** versus **connection-oriented** communication. The OSI model supports both connectionless and connection-oriented communication in the network layer, but only connection-oriented communication in the transport layer. The TCP/IP model has only one mode in the network layer (connectionless) but supports both modes in the transport layer.

Although the protocols associated with the OSI model are rarely used, the model itself is still valid. The TCP/IP model itself is not of much use but the protocols are widely used. In summary, the OSI model has proven to be exceptionally useful and the protocols of the TCP/IP are widely used for discussing computer networks. Every coin has two sides. ③ Generally, we use a modified OSI model but concentrate primarily on the TCP/IP and related protocols, and the **hybrid** model is shown in Figure 1.7.

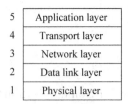

5	Application layer
4	Transport layer
3	Network layer
2	Data link layer
1	Physical layer

Figure 1.7   The hybrid reference model

Notes

① When computers or other terminal equipments exchange data，the procedures involved are quite complex. 这里 involved 动词的被动形式做形容词,修饰其前面的名词 procedures。翻译成"涉及的步骤……"或者"相关步骤……"。

② The entities comprising the corresponding layers on different machines are called peers. 这里 comprising the corresponding layers 整个短语一起修饰前面的 entities,翻译成"构成相应通信层的实体"。动词 comprising 是前面 entities 的谓语,而 corresponding layers 是 comprising 的宾语,comprising 动词的主动形式加 ing 做形容词修饰前面的名词。

③ Every coin has two sides. 意思是"喜忧参半"或者"任何事情都有两面性"。

New Words and Phrases

terminal	['tə:minl]	n.	末端;终点站;终点;终端机
exchange	[iks'tʃeindʒ]	v.	交换;兑换
procedure	[prə'si:dʒə]	n.	程序;手续;步骤
complexity	[kəm'pleksəti]	n.	复杂;复杂性;复杂的事物
break up into			分解
subtask	['sʌbtɑ:sk]	n.	程序子基元
stack	[stæk]	n.	堆;栈
interface	['intəfeis]	n.	界面;接口
adjacent	[ə'dʒeisnt]	adj.	邻近的;毗连的;接近的
peer	[piə]	n.	同辈;同等
correspond	[ˌkɔrə'spɔnd]	v.	符合;对应;通信
agreement	[ə'gri:mənt]	n.	同意;一致;协议
syntax	['sintæks]	n.	句法
semantics	[si'mæntiks]	n.	语义学;符号学
proposal	[prə'pəuzl]	n.	求婚;建议;提议
mechanical	[mi'kænikl]	adj.	机械的;力学的;呆板的
electrical	[i'lektrikl]	adj.	电的;与电有关的
characteristics	[ˌkæriktə'ristik]	n.	特性;特征;特点
functionality	[ˌfʌŋkʃə'næləti]	n.	功能;功能性

| hybrid | ［'haibrid］ | n. | 混合物；杂种；混血儿 |

Computer Terminologies

OSI reference model	OSI 参考模型
ISO(International Organization for Standardization)	国际标准化组织
frame	帧
synchronization	同步
congestion	阻塞
session	会话
token	令牌
general-purpose	通用的
session layer	会话层
presentation layer	表示层
HTTP(hyper text transfer protocol)	超文本传输协议
packet-switched	分组交换

Exercises

I. Translate these English sentences into Chinese.

1. It is clear that there must be a high degree of cooperation between two computer networks.

2. Most networks are organized as a stack of layers or levels, each one built upon the one below it, as shown in Figure 1. 4.

3. It is called the ISO OSI(Open Systems Interconnection) Reference Model because it deals with connecting open systems—that is, systems that are open for communication with other systems.

4. The design issues here deal with the mechanical, electrical, functional, and procedural characteristics to access the physical medium, which lies below the physical layer.

5. The main task of the data link layer is to provide for the reliable transfer of information across the physical link, including sending frames with the necessary synchronization, error control and flow control.

6. The processing unit of the network layer is the packet and its main functions are routing selection, congestion control and internetworking.

7. The basic function of the transport layer is to accept data from above, split it up into the smaller units if need be, pass these to the network layer, and ensure that the pieces all arrive correctly at the other end.

8. The application layer contains a variety of protocols that are commonly needed by users.

9. The TCP/IP model organizes the communication task into four independent layers: the host-to-network layer, the Internet layer, the transport layer, the application layer.

10. The OSI model supports both connectionless and connection-oriented communication in the network layer, but only connection-oriented communication in the transport layer. The TCP/IP model has only one mode in the network layer (connectionless) but supports both modes in the transport layer.

II. Answer the questions.

1. What kind of contents does network protocol mainly be studied?

2. How many layers are in the TCP/IP model and also OSI model? And describe the functions of each layer in both models.

3. Tell the differences between TCP/IP model and OSI model.

4. Why should the network model be divided into layers?

Extending Your Reading

What is the future of networking

The clearest part of the future network is that of nomadic computing and smart spaces. The available of lightweight, inexpensive, high-performance, portable computing devices plus the ubiquity of the Internet has enabled us to become nomads. Nomadic computing refers to the technology that enables end users who travel from place to place to gain access to Internet services in a transparent fashion, no matter where they travel. However, nomadic computing is only one step. The next step will enable us to move out from the netherworld of cyberspace to the physical world of smart spaces. The embedded technology will allow our environment to provide the IP services we want. When I walk into a room, the room will know I entered. I will be able to communicate with my environment naturally. Replies are generated by the Web pages presented on the wall and passed to me through as speech, holograms, and so forth.

参考译文

参 考 模 型

计算机或者其他终端设备之间交换数据涉及的步骤是相当复杂的。很显然,两个网络之间必须高度合作。为了减少设计的复杂性,将任务分解成子任务,其中每一个任务单独实现。大多数网络以多层形式组织,每一层的功能建立在它下面的一层之上,如图 1.4 所示。层的数量、每一层的名字、每一层的内容以及每一层的功能因网络的不同而不同。每一层为更高的一层提供特定的服务。在某种意义上,每一层像一种虚拟机。在每一对邻接层之间有一个接口,通过这个接口下面一层向它上面的一层提供服务。

当然,通信是在两台机器之间进行的。在不同机器上构成通信层的实体叫做对等实体。

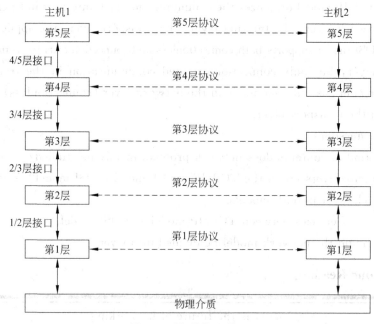

图 1.4　层、协议和接口

协议是通信双方之间如何进行通信的协定。一个协议主要的性质如下：

- 语法——数据块的格式。
- 语义——包括差错处理以及协作的控制信息。
- 定时——包括速度匹配和时序。

一般来说，我们把一套层的集合再加协议叫做网络的体系架构。两个重要的网络体系架构，即 OSI 参考模型和 TCP/IP 协议族，成为了标准化的框架。

OSI 参考模型

OSI 参考模型是由国际标准组织提出来的。之所以被称为国际标准组织的开放系统互连(ISO OSI)参考模型，是因为它负责处理开放系统之间的连接。所谓开放的系统，就是指系统可以与其他系统通信，简称 OSI 参考模型。

OSI 模型有七层，如图 1.5 所示。我们将要从最底层开始，依次讨论 OSI 模型的每一层。

物理层

物理层是在通信通道上传输原始比特流。这层的设计问题是处理接入位于物理层下的物理媒介的机械的、电气的、功能的以及程序化的特性。

数据链路层

数据链路层的主要功能是为信息在物理链路层上传输提供可靠性，包括帧发送同步、差错控制、流控制。数据链路层的处理单元是帧。

网络层

网络层控制子网的操作，是处理端到端传送的最低层。网络层的处理单元是包，它的主要功能是路由选择、拥塞控制以及网络互连。设计的主要问题之一是决定包如何从源节点

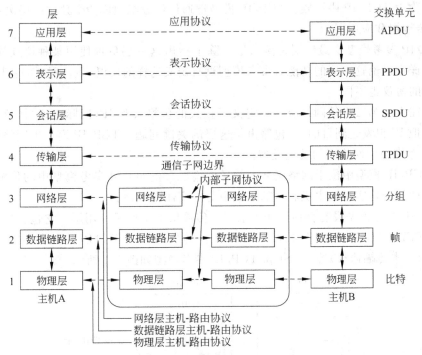

图 1.5   OSI 参考模型

路由到目的接点。为了达到这个目的，网络层必须了解通信子网的拓扑以及在考虑网络负载均衡时如何选择合适的路径通过。

传输层

传输层的基本功能是从上一层接收数据，如果需要的话，把它拆分成更小的数据单元传送给网络层，并且保证数据正确到达另一端。再者，所有这些必须高效地完成并且在一定程度上把高一层和物理技术上不可避免地改变隔离开。传输层是一个从源节点到目的节点的真正的端到端的层。

会话层

会话层允许不同机器上的用户在彼此之间建立会话。这一层提供多种服务，包括对话控制、令牌管理以及同步。

表示层

表示层关注的是信息传输的语法和语义。它管理抽象的数据结构和允许更高一层要定义和交换的数据结构。

应用层

应用层包含了很多用户需要的各种各样的协议。一种广泛使用的应用协议是超文本传输协议，它是万维网的基础。另外，像文件传输、电子邮件、多媒体这些通常的应用就位于这一层。

TCP/IP 参考模型

TCP/IP 体系架构是在实验的分组交换网 ARPANET 上进行协议研究和发展的结果，

它一般被称为 TCP/IP 协议族。TCP/IP 模型把通信任务组织成四个独立的层次：接入层、网络层、传输层和应用层。

TCP/IP 参考模型中最低层是接入层。除了指出这一层负责使用某种协议连接网络，这里先不详细讨论这一层的功能。参考模型没有定义这样的协议，而且不同的主机、不同的网络使用的协议也不同。

从下往上的第二层是网络层。它定义了正式的包格式和 IP（网际协议）协议。它的主要功能是把 IP 包发送到目的地，包路由是这层的关键问题。TCP/IP 模型中网络层的功能和 OSI 参考模型中网络层的功能类似。

在 TCP/IP 模型中位于网络层之上的是传输层。正如 OSI 参考模型中的传输层一样，这一层设计目的是实现源主机和目的主机中对等实体的对话。

TCP/IP 参考模型没有会话层和表示层。传输层的上面是应用层。它包含更高一层的协议，如 TELNET（远程登录协议）、FTP（文件传输协议）、SMTP（简单邮件传输协议）、HTTP（超文本传输协议）等。OSI 和 TCP/IP 参考模型如图 1.6 所示。

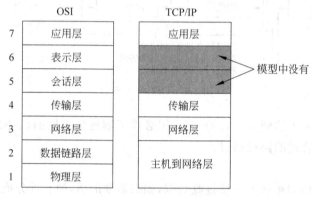

图 1.6　OSI 和 TCP/IP 参考模型

OSI 参考模型和 TCP/IP 参考模型的比较

OSI 参考模型和 TCP/IP 参考模型有很多的共同点。两者都是基于一个独立协议栈的概念。每一层的功能也大致类似。

尽管有这些相似之处，这两个模型仍然有很多不同的地方。

（1）OSI 参考模型中核心是三个概念：服务、接口、协议，但是 TCP/IP 参考模型最初并没有明确区分这三个概念。OSI 参考模型最大的贡献可能就是清楚区分了这三个概念。

（2）层的数量不同。OSI 参考模型有七层而 TCP/IP 参考模型只有四层。两者都有网络层、传输层和应用层，但是其他剩下的层不同。

（3）第三个不同点是无连接和面向连接通信这部分内容。OSI 模型在网络层支持两种通信连接方式，但是，在传输层只支持面向连接的通信方式。然而，TCP/IP 模型在网络层只支持面向无连接的通信模式，但是在传输层却支持两种通信模式。

虽然与 OSI 模型相关联的协议很少使用，但是模型本身仍然是有效的。TCP/IP 模型本身很少使用，但是其协议却被广泛使用。总之，在讨论计算机网络模型时，OSI 模型已被证明非常有用以及 TCP/IP 协议被广泛使用。任何事情都有两面性。通常，我们使用修正的 OSI 模型,并结合 TCP/IP 及相关协议,它们构成的混合模型如图 1.7 所示。

5	应用层
4	传输层
3	网络层
2	数据链路层
1	物理层

图 1.7　混合参考模型

Unit 2   The Physical Layer

Section A   Data Communication Basis

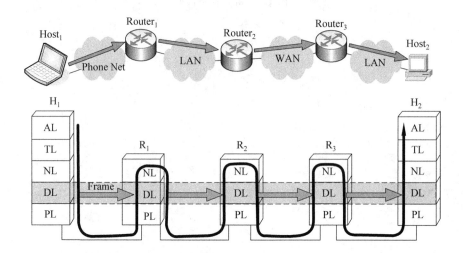

I. Introduction

The physical layer defines the mechanical, electrical, functional, and procedural characteristics to access the physical medium. We begin with a theoretical analysis of data transmission.

II. Concepts and Terminology

Data transmission occurs between transmitter and receiver over some transmission media. The transmission may be **simplex**, **half duplex** or **full duplex**. A connection that allows traffic in both directions **simultaneously** is called full duplex. [1] For example, a two-lane road is full duplex. A connection that allows traffic either way, but only one way at a time is called half duplex. In simplex transmission, the traffic is allowed in only one way.

According to the function of time, the **electromagnetic** signal may be classified into either **analog** or digital signals, as shown in Figure 2. 1. An **analog signal** is one in which the signal intensity varies in a smooth fashion over time. There are no breaks in the analog signal. A **digital signal** is one in which the signal **intensity** maintains a constant level for some period of time and then changes to another constant level. [2]

The **amplitude**, frequency, or phase of a **sine** wave **carrier** can be **modulated** to transmit information. In **amplitude modulation** (**AM**), two different amplitudes are used to represent 0 and 1, respectively. **Frequency modulation**, also known as frequency shift

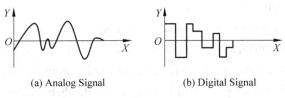

(a) Analog Signal　　　　(b) Digital Signal

Figure 2.1　Analog and digital signal

keying(**FSK**), uses two (or more) different tones. In the simplest form of **phase modulation**, or phase shift keying(PSK), the carrier wave is systematically shifted 0 or 180 degrees at uniformly spaced intervals. The new modulation techniques **QPSK**, **QAM-16**, **QAM**-64 are widely used.

The range of frequencies transmitted without being strongly **attenuated** is called the bandwidth, expressed in Hz. The bandwidth is a physical property of the transmission medium and usually depends on the construction, thickness, and length of the medium.

In the telephone system, the **multiplexing** schemes are used to maintain a high-bandwidth for users with low costs. These multiplexing schemes are **FDM** (Frequency Division Multiplexing), **TDM** (Time Division Multiplexing), **WDM** (Wavelength Division Multiplexing), **CDMA**(Code Division Multiple Access). In FDM, the frequency spectrum is divided into frequency bands, some of which is used by each user having **exclusively**. In TDM, the users take turns getting the entire bandwidth for a little burst of time periodically.

III. Channel Capacity

As early as 1924, Henry Nyquist realized that even a perfect channel has a finite transmission capacity. He derived an equation expressing the maximum data rate for a finite bandwidth noiseless channel. In 1948, Claude Shannon carried Nyquist's work further and extended it to the case of a random noise channel.

1. Nyquist Bandwidth

To begin with, the case of a channel that is noise free[3] is considered. Nyquist proved that if an **arbitrary** signal has been run through a low-pass filter of bandwidth B, the filtered signal can be completely reconstructed by making only 2B (exact) samples[4] per second. Sampling the line faster than $2B$ times per second is pointless because the higher frequency will be filtered out. For example, a noiseless channel with a bandwidth of 3100 Hz can transmit binary signals at the maximum rate 6200 bps. If the signal consists of M **discrete** levels, the Nyquist **formulation** becomes:

$$C = 2B\log_2 M \quad \text{bits/sec} \tag{2.1}$$

According to the formula (2.1), the data rate can be increased by increasing the number of different signal elements. But it is not the case. Noise and other impairments on the transmission line will limit the practical value of M.

2. Shannon Theorem

The Nyquist formula has considered only noiseless channels[⑤]. If random noise is present, the situation **deteriorates** rapidly. The amount of thermal noise present is measured by the ratio of the signal power to the noise power, called the **signal-to-noise ratio** (SNR, or S/N). Usually, the ratio is given in **decibels** (dB), expressed in formula (2.2):

$$\text{SNR}_{dB} = 10\lg \frac{\text{signal power}}{\text{noise power}} \tag{2.2}$$

For example, a ratio of 100 is 20 dB.

The signal-to-noise ratio is important in the transmission of digital data because it sets the upper bound on the achievable data rate. Shannon's major result is that the maximum data rate of a noisy channel obeys the equation (2.3):

$$C = B\log_2(1+S/N) \quad \text{bits/sec} \tag{2.3}$$

Where C is the capacity of the channel in bits per second and B is the bandwidth of the channel in Hz. For example, a channel of 1MHz bandwidth with a signal-to-noise ratio of 20dB can never transmit much more than 6.66Mbps, no matter how many signal levels are used. The Shannon formula represents the theoretical maximum that can be achieved. In practice, only much lower rates are achieved.

Notes

① A connection that allows traffic in both directions simultaneously is called full duplex. 这里的 that 引导一个定语从句修饰 connection，connection 在主句和从句中都做主语。

② A digital signal is one in which the signal intensity maintains a constant level for some period of time and then changes to another constant level. 这里由 which 引导一个定语从句，one 指代前面的 digital signal，实际这个句子应该是"The signal intensity maintains a constant level for some period of time and then changes to another constant level in digital signal"。

③ noise free 这里解释为"无噪声的"。

④ by making only 2B (exact) samples 这里解释为"以 2B 频率采样"。

⑤ noiseless channels 这里解释为"无噪声的信道"。

New Words and Phrases

simplex	['simpleks]	*n.*	单工
simultaneously	[ˌsiməl'teiniəsli]	*adv.*	同时地
electromagnetic	[iˌlektrəumæg'netik]	*adj.*	电磁的
analog	['ænəlɔːg]	*adj.*	模拟的；类比的
intensity	[in'tensəti]	*n.*	强度；强烈；紧张
amplitude	['æmplituːd]	*n.*	广阔；充足；丰富；[物]振幅

phase	[feiz]	n.	相位;方面;局面;阶段;时期
sine	[sain]	n.	正弦
carrier	[ˈkæriə]	n.	航空母舰;带菌者;运送者
modulate	[ˈmɔdjuleit]	v.	调整;调节(声音);变调
attenuate	[əˈtenjueit]	v.	变细;稀释;变弱
multiplexing	[ˈmʌltipleksiŋ]	v.	多路传输
arbitrary	[ˈɑːbitrəri]	adj.	任意的;专制的;武断的
discrete	[diˈskriːt]	adj.	不连续的;分离的
formulation	[fɔːmjuˈleiʃn]	n.	公式化;规划;构想;配方
deteriorate	[diˈtiəriəreit]	v.	恶化;变质;衰退
decibel	[ˈdesibel]	n.	分贝(音量的单位)

Computer Terminologies

half duplex	半双工
full duplex	全双工
analog signal	模拟信号
digital signal	数字信号
amplitude modulation（AM）	调幅
Frequency modulation(FM)	调频
frequency shift keying(FSK)	移频键控
phase modulation(PM)	调相
phase shift keying(PSK)	移相键控
QPSK(Quadrature phase shift keying)	四相移键控
QAM（Quadrature Amplitude Modulation）	正交调幅
bandwidth	带宽
FDM(Frequency Division Multiplexing)	频分复用
TDM(Time Division Multiplexing)	时分复用
WDM(Wavelength Division Multiplexing)	波分复用
CDMA(Code Division Multiple Access)	码分多址
signal-to-noise ratio（SNR，or S/N）	信噪比

Exercises

I. Answer the questions.

1. What may be the maximum data rate in a noiseless binary channel with a bandwidth of 1000Hz?

2. Can you give the SNR ratio of 1000 expressed in dB?

3. Can you derive the maximum data rate in a noisy channel of 2MHz bandwidth with signal-to-noise ratio of 30dB according to the Shannon formula? And what is it?

II. Match each numbered item with the most closely related lettered item. Write your answers in the spaces provided.

a. signal-to-noise ratio   1. (   ) allows traffic in both directions simultaneously.

b. digital signal   2. An (   ) is one in which the signal intensity varies in a smooth fashion over time.

c. full duplex.   3. the ratio of the signal power to the noise power, called the (   )

d. analog signal   4. A (   ) is one in which the signal intensity maintains a constant level for some period of time and then changes to another constant level.

Extending Your Reading

Case history—Public WiFi access

Only five years ago, wireless computing networks were somewhat of an oddity. Although massive investment was pouring into licensing radio spectrum for 3G systems, 3G systems were only at early stages of deployment. Today, many corporations, universities, and homes have their own wireless IEEE 802.11 LANs. Even more remarkably, the number of wireless hot spots—public locations where users can find 802.11 wireless access—is rapidly expanding. What a difference five years can make! The dream of nearly ubiquitous, anytime, seamless access to the global Internet may be closer.

参考译文

数据通信基础

物理层定义了接入物理介质的机械的、电气的、功能性的、程序化的特征。我们从分析数据传输的理论开始。

概念和术语

数据传输是在发送者与接收者之间通过传输媒介进行。数据传输可能是单工、半双工、全双工。允许两个方向同时进行的通信叫做全双工通信。例如,一条两车道的公路是全双工。两个方向都可以同时通信,但是一次只能一个方向的叫做半双工。单工只允许一个方向通信。

根据时间函数电磁信号可分类为模拟信号和数字信号,如图 2.1 所示。模拟信号是信号强度随着时间平滑变化。模拟信号中间没有间断。数字信号是指信号强度在一段时间维持一个恒定水平,而在另一段时间维持另一个恒定水平。

一个正弦载波的振幅、频率或者相位可以调制用来传输信息。在调幅中,两个不同的振幅分别用来表示 0 和 1。调频,也称为频移键控,使用两个或多个不同的频率。调相,也称

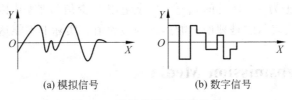

(a) 模拟信号　　　　　　　　(b) 数字信号

图 2.1　模拟信号和数字信号

相移键控,其最简单的形式是载波以均匀的空间间隔整体移位 0 度或者 180 度。新的调制技术 QPSK、QAM-16、QAM-64 也被广泛使用。

信号没有明显衰减的传输频率范围叫做带宽,用赫兹表示。带宽是传输媒介的物理属性,经常依赖于物理介质的结构、直径以及长度。

电话系统中,多路复用为用户以低成本来维持高带宽。这些多路复用模式有频分多路复用(FDM)、时分多路复用(TDM)、波分多路复用(WDM)、码分多址(CDMA)。FDM 中的频谱分为多个频段,其中某一些频段为每一个用户单独占有。在 TDM 中,用户按周期地分时间片轮流占用整个带宽。

信道容量

早在 1924 年,亨利·奈奎斯特就认识到即使是一个完美的信道也只拥有有限的传输容量。他推导出一个公式用来表示无噪声信道有限带宽的最大传输速率。在 1948 年,克劳德·香农把奈奎斯特的工作进一步扩展到任意的有噪声信道。

奈奎斯特带宽

首先只考虑无噪声信道的情况。奈奎斯特证明如果一个任意的信号穿过一个带宽为 B 的低通滤波器,只要以每秒 2 倍 B(要求精确的)次采样,被过滤掉的信号完全可以被重新构造。以多于每秒 $2B$ 次采样是无意义的因为高频率部分会被过滤掉。例如,一个带宽为 3100 赫兹的无噪声信道能够以最大速率为每秒 6200 比特传输二进制信号。如果信号包含 M 个离散值,奈奎斯特公式如 2.1 所示:

$$最大传输速率\ C = 2B\log_2 M\ 比特/秒 \tag{2.1}$$

根据公式(2.1),可以通过增加不同信号元素的数量来提高数据速率。但这不是问题所在。传输线路的噪声和其他损害将会限制 M 的实际值。

香农定理

奈奎斯特公式只考虑无噪声信道。如果允许存在任意的噪声,情况迅速恶化。存在的热噪声数量可以通过信号功率与噪声功率的比值来衡量。叫做信噪比(SNR 或者 S/N)。通常这个比值用分贝(dB)来衡量,公式如 2.2 所示:

$$信噪比_{分贝} = 10\lg \frac{信号功率}{噪声功率} \tag{2.2}$$

例如,信噪比为 100 是 20 分贝。

信噪比在数字数据传输中是很重要的,因为它设置了一个可以达到的速率的上限值。香农的主要成果是噪声信道的最大速率遵守公式(2.3):

$$最大速率\ C = B\log_2(1 + 信号功率/噪声功率)\ 比特/秒 \tag{2.3}$$

C 是信道的最大传输速率,单位是比特/秒,B 是信道的带宽,单位是赫兹。比如,一个带宽为1MHz,信噪比为 20 分贝的信道,不管使用多少信号值,其传输速率最高不超过 6.66Mbps。香农公式表示的是理论上能达到的最大值。实际上不能达到最高速率值。

Section B Transmission Media

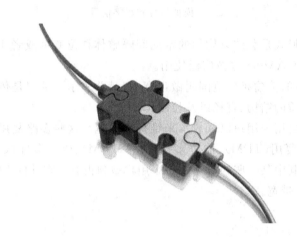

I. Introduction

Transmission media are roughly grouped into guided and unguided media. With guided media, the waves are transmitted along the physical path. Guided media are the **twisted pair**, the **coaxial cable** and the **optic fiber**. Unguided media, also called wireless, provides a means for electromagnetic waves, such as the radio, the infrared wave.

II. Guided Transmission Media

1. Twisted Pair

The least expensive and most widely used guided transmission medium is twisted pair. A twisted pair consists of two **insulated copper** wires arranged in a **helical** form, typically about 1mm thick. A wire pair acts as a single communication link. When the wires are twisted, the waves from different twists cancel out, so the wire radiates less effectively. Commonly, a number of these pairs are bundled together into a cable by wrapping them in a tough protective **sheath**. [①]

The most common application of the twisted pair is the telephone system. Twisted pairs can run several kilometers without **amplification**, but for longer distances, **repeaters** are needed. Twisted pairs can be used for transmitting either analog or digital signals. The bandwidth depends on the thickness of the wire and the distance traveled.

Twisted pair comes in two varieties: unshielded and **shielded**, as shown in Figure 2.2. Unshielded twisted pair (**UTP**) is ordinary telephone wire. It is also used for local area networks and is easy to work and install. UTP has two standards: EIA-568-A and EIA-568-B, published by the **Electronic Industries Cabling Standard**. The order of these two standards is as follows:

EIA-568-A: green-white, green, orange-white, blue, blue-white, orange, brown-white, brown

EIA-568-B: orange-white, orange, green-white, blue, blue-white, green, brown-white, brown

Of these, category 3 and category 5 UTP cable have received the most attention for LAN applications. Category 5 is more expensive but provides much better performance than Category 3.

Shielded twisted pair (STP) provides better performance and higher data rates but is more expensive and more difficult to work than UTP.

Figure 2.2　UTP and STP

2. Coaxial Cable

Another common transmission medium is the coaxial cable. It has better shielding than twisted pairs and can span longer distances at higher speeds. It is a good combination of high bandwidth and excellent noise **immunity**. There are two kinds of coaxial cable widely used: 50-**ohm** and 75-ohm. The 50-ohm cable is commonly used for digital transmission, and the 75-ohm cable is for analog transmission and cable television.

A coaxial cable consists of a stiff copper wire as the core, surrounded by an insulating material. The insulator is encased by a cylindrical conductor, and the outer conductor is covered in a protective plastic sheath. A coaxial cable is shown in Figure 2.3.

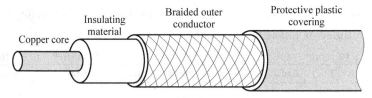

Figure 2.3　Coaxial cable

3. Optic Fiber

An optical fiber is a flexible medium capable of guiding an optical **ray**. Various glasses and plastics can be used to make optical fibers. The optical fiber cable has a cylindrical shape and consists of three key components: the light source, the transmission medium, and the detector. Optical fiber transmits a signal-encoded **beam** of light by means of total internal **reflection**. When a light ray **bumps** on the boundary above the **critical angle**, it will be reflected internally and many different rays will be **bounced** around at different angles. [2] Each ray is said to have a different mode. The fiber having this property is called a

multimode fiber. However, if the fiber's diameter is reduced to a few wavelengths of light, the fiber acts like a wave guide, and the light can **propagate** only in a straight line, without bouncing, **yielding** a single-mode fiber, as shown in Figure 2.4. Single-mode fibers are more expensive but are widely used for longer distances. Currently available single-mode fibers can transmit data at 50Gbps for 100km without amplification.

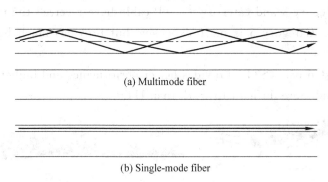

(a) Multimode fiber

(b) Single-mode fiber

Figure 2.4 Multimode fiber and single-mode fiber

Compared with twisted pair or coaxial cable, optical fiber has the following characteristics: much higher bandwidth, longer communication distance, smaller size and lighter weight. Furthermore, fibers do not **leak** light and are quite difficult to **tap**. These give fibers excellent security.

III. Wireless Transmission

If people need to be on-line all the time, it is the most appropriate choice for mobile users to use wireless transmission. The electromagnetic wave is propagated through space and the electromagnetic **spectrum** is shown in Figure 2.5. The **radio, microwave,** and **infrared** of the spectrum can all be used for transmitting information by modulating the frequency, amplitude, or phase of the waves.

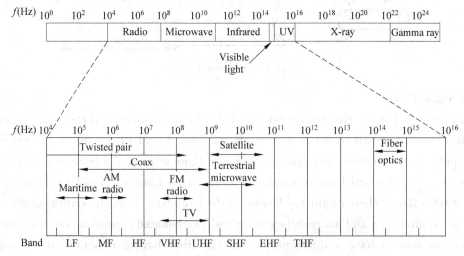

Figure 2.5 The electromagnetic spectrum and its uses for communication

1. Radio Transmission

Radio waves with frequencies in the range of 30MHz to 1GHz are suitable for **omni-directional** applications, including indoors and outdoors. It is easy to generate, can travel long distances, and can **penetrate** buildings easily.

2. Microwave Transmission

Frequencies in the range of about 1GHz to 40GHz are referred to as microwave frequencies. Unlike radio waves at lower frequencies, microwaves do not pass through buildings well. The microwave is suitable for point-to-point transmission, and is widely used for long-distance telephone communication, television distribution, mobile phones and satellite communications.

3. Infrared Waves

Infrared is widely used for local point-to-point and multipoint communications within short-range areas, such as a single room. The infrared is relatively directional, cheap, and easy to build, but does not pass through solid objects.

4. Communication Satellites

The communication satellite is an **artificial** satellite used to aid **telecommunications** by reflecting or relaying a radio signal. Each satellite connects two or more microwave sending/receiving station on the earth. According to the **altitude** of the satellite, there are three kinds of satellite: **geostationary satellites**, medium-earth orbit (**MEO**) satellites and **low-earth orbit satellites**. Geostationary satellites are used for long-distance communications and have a propagation delay of roughly 3μsec/km. Medium-earth orbit satellites are not used for telecommunications. The GPS (Global Positioning System) satellites orbiting at about 18,000km are examples of MEO satellites. Because low-earth orbit satellites are close to the earth, they don't need much power with high speed and low delay. Due to their rapid motion, they commonly have a complete system, such as the **iridium** system.

Notes

① Commonly, a number of these pairs are bundled together into a cable by wrapping them in a tough protective sheath. 这里的 them 指代的是 a number of these pairs, 多对双绞线对被一起绑定在一层坚硬的保护套里。

② When a light ray bumps on the boundary above the critical angle, it will be reflected internally and many different rays will be bounced around at different angles. 这里的 it 指代前面的 ligth ray 光束。当光线超过临界角,它将发生内反射,光束以不同的角度传输出去。

New Words and Phrases

insulate	['insjuleit]	vt.	使绝缘;隔离
copper	['kɔpə]	n.	铜;铜币;警察;紫铜色

helical	['helikl]	adj.	螺旋状的
sheath	[ʃiːθ]	n.	鞘;护套
amplification	[ˌæmplifi'keiʃən]	n.	扩大;放大(率);放大倍数
shield	[ʃiːld]	vt.	保护;庇护
immunity	[i'mjuːnəti]	n.	免疫;免疫性;免除
ohm	[əum]	n.	欧姆(电阻单位);欧姆(物理学家)
stiff	[stif]	adj.	硬的;艰难的;生硬的;拘谨的
hollow	['hɔləu]	adj.	空的;空洞的;凹陷的
cylindrical	[sə'lindrikl]	adj.	圆柱形的
conductor	[kən'dʌktə]	n.	售票员;导体;指挥
plastic	['plæstik]	n.	塑料;塑料制品;信用卡
ray	[rei]	n.	光线;射线;辐射
beam	[biːm]	n.	光线;(光线的)束
reflection	[ri'flekʃən]	n.	倒影;反射;反映
bump	[bʌmp]	v.	碰撞;颠簸而行;提高
critical angle			临界角
bounce	[bauns]	vi.	弹起;重新恢复;退票
propagate	['prɔpəgeit]	v.	繁殖;传播;传送
yield	[jiːld]	v.	生产;获利;屈服
leak	[liːk]	v.	渗;漏;泄露
tap	[tæp]	v.	开发;利用;索要;装龙头;窃听
spectrum	['spektrəm]	n.	范围;光谱;[科]频谱
omni-directional	[ˌɔmnidə'rekʃənl]	adj.	全方位的
penetrate	['penətreit]	v.	渗透;穿透;(情报人员的)渗透
artificial	[ˌɑːti'fiʃl]	adj.	人造的;虚伪的;武断的
telecommunication	[ˌtelikəˌmjuːni'keiʃn]	n.	电信;远程通信
altitude	['æltituːd]	n.	高度;海拔;高地
iridium	[i'ridiəm]	n.	铱

Computer Terminologies

twisted pair	双绞线
coaxial cable	同轴电缆
optic fiber	光纤
UTP	非屏蔽双绞线
Repeater	中继器
Electronic Industries Cabling Standard	电子工业布线标准
STP	屏蔽双绞线
multimode fiber	多模光纤
single-mode fiber	单模光纤

radio	无线电
microwave	微波
infrared	红外线
geostationary satellites	地球静止轨道通信卫星
MEO (medium-earth orbit satellites)	中轨道卫星
low-earth orbit satellites	低轨道卫星
GPS(Global Positioning System)	全球定位系统

Exercises

I. Fill in the blanks.

Use the listed words to fill in the bracket: *unguided*, *twisted pair*, *copper*, *radiates*, *telephone system*, *amplification*, *repeaters*, *analog*, *unshielded*, *coaxial cable*, *An optical fiber*, *multimode fiber*, *single-mode fiber*, *wireless*, *Radio*, *pass through*, *Infrared*, *artificial*, *telecommunications*.

Transmission media are roughly grouped into guided and (　　) media.

The least expensive and most widely used guided transmission medium is (　　). A twisted pair consists of two insulated (　　) wires arranged in a helical form, typically about 1mm thick. A wire pair acts as a single communication link. When the wires are twisted, the waves from different twists are cancelled out, so the wire (　　) less effectively. The most common application of the twisted pair is the (　　). Twisted pairs can run several kilometers without (　　), but for longer distances, (　　) are needed. Twisted pairs can be used for transmitting either (　　) or digital signals. The bandwidth depends on the thickness of the wire and the distance traveled. Twisted pair comes in two varieties: (　　) and shielded. Another common transmission medium is the (　　). It is a good combination of high (　　) and excellent noise immunity. There are two kinds of coaxial cable widely used: 50-ohm and 75-ohm. (　　) is a flexible medium capable of guiding an optical ray. The optical fiber cable has a cylindrical shape and consists of three key components: the light source, the transmission medium, and the detector. There are two kinds of optical fiber: (　　), (　　).

Unguided media, also called wireless, provides a means for electromagnetic waves, such as the radio, the infrared wave. If people need to be on-line all the time, it is the most appropriate choice for mobile users to use (　　) transmission. (　　) waves with frequencies in the range of 30MHz to 1GHz are suitable for omni-directional applications, including indoors and outdoors. Frequencies in the range of about 1GHz to 40GHz are referred to as microwave frequencies. Unlike radio waves at lower frequencies, microwaves do not (　　) buildings well. (　　) is widely used for local point-to-point and multipoint communications within short-range areas, such as a single room. The communication satellite is an (　　) satellite used to aid (　　) by reflecting or relaying a radio signal. Each satellite connects two or more microwave sending/receiving station on the earth.

II. Answer the questions.

1. List the line order of the EIA-568-A.

2. List the all transmission media that you know.

Extending Your Reading

An interview with Charlie Perkins

Charles E. Perkins is a Nokia Fellow in the Communication system Laboratory at Nokia Research Center, investigating mobile wireless networking and dynamic configuration protocols. He is the editor of several ACM and IEEE journals for areas related to wireless networking. He serves as document editor for the mobile-IP working group of the Internet Engineering Task Force(IETF), and has written or co-written standards-track documents in the moibleip, manet, IPv6, and seamless mobility working group.

参考译文

传 输 介 质

传输媒体大致分成有导向的介质和无导向的介质。对于有导向的介质,例如双绞线、同轴电缆以及光纤,光波沿着物理路径进行传输。无导向的介质也叫无线介质,例如无线电波、红外波,为电磁波提供了传输介质。

有导向传输介质

双绞线

使用最广泛价格最便宜的有导向传输介质是双绞线。双绞线由两根绝缘的同轴电线呈螺旋状绞在一起,通常直径约 1 毫米。每一对电线构成单一的通信链路。当电线被绞合在一起时,不同电线产生的波相互抵消,所以电线的辐射就会显著减弱。通常,很多对这样的双绞线被包裹在一个坚硬的保护层里,一起绑定到一根电缆里。

双绞线最常见的应用是电话系统。双绞线在没有放大的情况下可以传输几千米,但如果超出这个距离就需要中继器。双绞线既可以用来传输模拟信号又可以用来传输数字信号。带宽取决于电线的直径和传输的距离。

双绞线分两类:屏蔽双绞线和非屏蔽双绞线,如图 2.2 所示。普通的电话线就是非屏蔽双绞线。它也使用于局域网,易于加工和安装。非屏蔽双绞线有 EIA-568-A 和 EIA-568-B 两个标准,由电子工业布线标准颁布的。这两个标准的线序如下:

EIA-568-A:绿白,绿,橙白,蓝,蓝白,橙,棕白,棕

EIA-568-B:橙白,橙,绿白,蓝,蓝白,绿,棕白,棕

非屏蔽 3 类和 5 类双绞线在局域网应用受到了最多的关注。5 类双绞线比 3 类的性能更好一些,价格也贵一些。

图 2.2　非屏蔽双绞线和屏蔽双绞线

比起非屏蔽双绞线,屏蔽双绞线提供更好的性能更高的速率,但是价格贵一些,也更难加工。

同轴电缆

另外一种常用的传输媒介是同轴电缆。比起双绞线,它有更好的屏蔽效果,可以以更快的速率传输更远的距离。它结合了高带宽和优秀的抗噪能力。有两类同轴电缆被广泛使用:50Ω 和 75Ω。50Ω 电缆经常用于数字信号传输,75Ω 电缆经常用于模拟信号传输和有线电视。

同轴电缆以硬铜线为芯,外面包裹着一层绝缘材料。绝缘层的外面由一个圆柱导体包围,导体外面覆盖了一层塑料保护层。同轴电缆如图 2.3 所示。

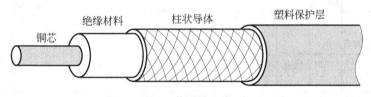

图 2.3　同轴电缆

光纤

光纤是一种可以引导光学射线的弹性介质。各种各样的玻璃和塑料可以用来制作光纤。光纤电缆有一个圆柱的形状,由三个主要部分组成:光源、传输介质和检测器。光纤以全内反射的方式传输已编码的光信号。当光束落在临界角以上的边界时,它将在内部反射,许多的光束将以不同角度反射出去。可以说每一束光有一个不同的模式。有这个性质的光纤叫多模光纤。虽然如此,如果光纤的直径减少到光的波长几倍,光纤就作为一个波导,光线只能以直线传播,没有发散,这就是如图 2.4 所示的单模光纤。单模光纤贵很多,但是更广泛地使用于远距离。目前,可用的单模光纤在没有放大的情况下,以 50Gbps 的速度传输 100km。

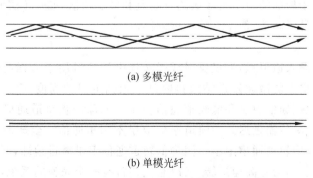

(a) 多模光纤

(b) 单模光纤

图 2.4　多模光纤和单模光纤

与双绞线或者同轴电缆相比,光纤有以下特点:更高的带宽、更远的通信距离、更小的体积和更轻的重量。再者,光纤不漏光,很难窃听。这使得光纤具有非常高的安全性。

无线传输

如果人们想要时刻在线,移动用户最合适的选择就是使用无线传输。电磁波可在空间中传输,电磁波谱如图 2.5 所示。通过调制电波的频率、振幅或者相位,无线电、微波和红外线能够用来传输信息。

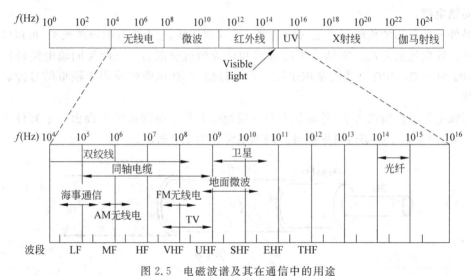

图 2.5　电磁波谱及其在通信中的用途

无线电传输

频率在 30MHz 到 1GHz 范围的无线电适合室内外的全方位应用。它容易产生,能传输很远的距离,能轻易地穿透建筑物。

微波传输

频率在 1GHz 到 40GHz 的,是微波频率。不像低频的无线电波,微波不能很好地穿过建筑物。微波适合点对点传输,可以被广泛用于长途电话通信、电视转播、移动电话和卫星通信。

红外线

红外线广泛用于局部的短距离区域的点对点和多点通信,如一个房间。相对来说,红外线有方向性、便宜,易于制造,但是不能穿过固体。

通信卫星

通信卫星是一颗人造卫星,通过反射或者转播电波信号用于远程通信。每一颗卫星连接地面上两个或者更多的微波发送站或接收站。根据卫星的高度,有三类卫星:地球静止轨道通信卫星、中轨道通信卫星和低轨道通信卫星。地球静止轨道通信卫星用于远距离通信,大约每公里有 $3\mu s$ 传输延迟。中轨道通信卫星不用于通信。全球地位系统卫星轨道大约在 1.8 万公里,是中轨道通信卫星。因为低轨道通信卫星靠近地球,所以不需要很多的能量且高速度低延迟。因为它高速运转,所以它们通常有一个完整的系统,例如铱系统。

Section C   Circuit Switching and Packet Switching

I. Introduction

The computer network consists of the communication subnet and the resource subnet, in which the communication subnet is the core of the Internet. ① The communication in the Internet is implemented by using packet switching. Nowadays, there are two different switching techniques used: **circuit switching** and **packet switching**. We will go into circuit switching and packet switching how they work **in detail**.

II. Circuit Switching

In a circuit-switching network, a **dedicated** communication path is established between two ends before communication begins. The path is the **sequence** of physical links connecting between nodes. ② Once the path is establish, data generated by the source station are transmitted along the path as rapidly as possible. At each node on the path, **incoming** data are routed or switched to the appropriate outgoing line without delay. The most common example of circuit switching is the telephone network.

III. Packet Switching

Compared with circuit switching, packet switching is a quite different approach. It uses **store-and-forward** transmission and is not necessary to setup an **end-to-end** path through the network. Rather, data are sent out in packets and the first packet can just be sent as soon as possible. At each node, the entire packet is received, stored briefly and then transmitted to the next node selected independently.

The differences between circuit switching and packet switching are shown in Figure 2. 6.

Item	Circuit-switched	Packet-switched
Call setup	Required	Not needed
Dedicated physical path	Yes	No
Each packet follows the same route	Yes	No
Packets arrive in order	Yes	No
Is a swich crash fatal	Yes	No
Bandwidth available	fixed	Dynamic
When can congestion occur	At setup time	On every packet
Potentially wasted bandwidth	Yes	No
Store-and-forward transmission	No	Yes
Transparency	Yes	No
Charging	Per minute	Per packet

Figure 2.6　Comparison of circuit switching and packet switching

Notes

① The computer network consists of the communication subnet and the resource subnet，in which the communication subnet is the core of the Internet，这里的 which 引导一个定语从句，指代的是 computer network。

② The path is the sequence of physical links connecting between nodes. 这里的 connecting 的主语是 physical links，connecting between nodes 一起修饰前面的 links，意思是，通信路径指的是连接节点间的物理链路所构成的序列。

New Words and Phrases

in detail			详细地
dedicate	['dedikeit]	vt.	致力于；献出；题献辞
sequence	['si:kwəns]	n.	顺序；连续；次序；一系列
incoming	['inkʌmiŋ]	adj.	进来的，回来的；

Computer Terminologies

circuit switching	电路交换
packet switching	分组交换
store-and-forward	存储转发
end-to-end	端到端

Exercises

I. Answer the questions.

1. Describe the differences between circuit switching and packet switching.

2. What is the most common application of circuit switching?

II. Fill in the blanks with these words *circuit switching*，*store-and-forward*，*transmitted*，*communication subnet*，*telephone network*，*packet switching*.

1. Nowadays，there are two different switching techniques used：(　　) and (　　).

2. Packet switching uses (　　) transmission.

3. The most common example of circuit switching is the (　　).

4. The computer network consists of the (　　) and the resource subnet，in which the communication subnet is the core of the Internet.

5. At each node，the entire packet is received，stored briefly and then (　　) to the next node selected independently.

Extending Your Reading

Case history—Development of packet switching

Three research groups around the world，all unaware of the others' work，began inventing the notion of packet switching as an efficient and robust alternative to circuit switching. The first published work on packet-switching techniques was the work by Leonard Kleinrock，at that time a graduate student at MIT. Using queuing theory，Kleinrock's work elegantly demonstrated the effectiveness of the packet-switching approach for bursty traffic sources. At the same time，Paul Baran at the Rand Institute had begun investigating the use of packet switching for secure voice over military networks，while at the National Physical Laboratory in England，Donald Davies and Roger Scantlebury were also developing their ideas on packet switching. The work at MIT，Rand，and NPL laid the foundations for today's Internet.

参考译文

电路交换和分组交换

计算机网络由通信子网和资源子网构成，其中通信子网是因特网的核心。因特网的通信由分组交换实现。现今，使用的有两种不同的交换技术：电路交换和分组交换。我们将要详细地研究电路交换和分组交换是如何工作的。

电路交换

电路交换网络中，在通信开始之前，先要在两端建立专用的通信路径。通信路径是节点之间形成的物理链路的序列。一旦通信路径形成之后，由源端产生的数据被尽可能快地发送出去。在通信路径的每一个节点，收到的数据无延迟地路由或者交换到合适的外面的线路。电路交换最常用的例子就是电话网络。

分组交换

分组交换是一种与电路交换完全不同的通信方式。它使用存储转发的发送方式，没有必要建立一条通过网络的端到端的通信路径。而是数据以包的形式发送出去,第一个包以最快的速度发送出去。在每一个节点,整个包被接收,进行简单存储,然后传输给独立选择的下一个节点。

分组交换和电路交换的不同之处如图 2.6 所示。

名　　称	电路交换	分组交换
线路建立	需要	不需要
专门的物理路径	有	没有
每个分组沿着相同的路由	是	不是
分组按序到达	是	否
一台交换机崩溃是否有严重影响	有	无
可用带宽	固定	动态
拥塞出现时刻	线路建立时刻	每个分组传输时刻
可能浪费带宽	是	否
存储-转发机制	否	是
透明性	是	否
收费	每分钟	每个分组

图 2.6　电路交换与分组交换的比较

Unit 3　The Data Link Layer

Section A　Error Detection and Correction

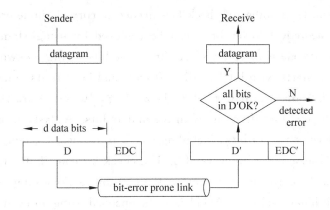

I. Introduction

The main functions of the data link layer include providing a well-defined service interface to the network layer, dealing with transmission errors, and regulating the data flow. Providing reliable transfer for information across the physical link is the most important task. Now there are two strategies developed for dealing with errors: **Hamming code** and **CRC**. The former is **error-correcting codes**, and the latter is **error-detecting codes**. Let us study each of these in turn.

II. Hamming code

1. Hamming distance

Normally, a frame consists of m data bits and r **redundant** bits. The redundant bits are used for checking or correcting errors. An n-bit ($n = m + r$) unit containing data and check bits is often referred to as an n-bit **codeword**.

Given any two codewords, 10001001 and 10110001, it is possible to determine how many corresponding bits differ. In this case, 3 bits differ. The number of bit positions in which two codewords differ is called the Hamming distance. It can be achieved by using **exclusive OR**. [1]

2. Parity Checks

Suppose the information to be sent, D, has d bits. In an even parity scheme, the sender simply includes one additional bit and chooses its value such that the total number of 1 in the d+1 bits is even. That is to say, if the number of 1 in the original information plus a bit of **parity** is **even**, it is called even checking. Similarly, for **odd** parity schemes, the parity bit value is chosen such that there are an odd number of 1's. For example, when 1011011 is sent in even parity, a bit is added to the end to make it 10110111. With odd parity 1001010 becomes 10010100.

3. Hamming Encoding

Assume that a code with m message bits and r check bits will allow all single errors to be corrected. Using $n=m+r$, there is the requirement of $(m+r+1) \leqslant 2^r$. Given m, it puts a **lower limit** on the number of check bits needed to correct single errors.

In fact, the **theoretical** lower limit can be achieved by using Hamming code. The method of Hamming code is as follows. At first, the bits of the codeword are numbered **continuously**, which starts with bit 1 at the left end, and bit 2 to its immediate right, and so on. Then, the bits that are **powers** of 2 (1, 2, 4, 8, 16, etc.) are check bits and the rest (3, 5, 6, 7, 9, etc.) are filled up with the m data bits. At last, each check bit forces the parity of some collection of bits, including itself, to be even (or odd). The number of data bits rewrites k as a sum of powers of 2. If a check bit contributes to the data bit, it may be included in the parity computation of the data bit[②]. For example, $11=1+2+8$. An 8-bit byte with binary value 10101111 is to be encoded using an even-parity Hamming code. The binary value after encoding is 101001001111.

III. Error-detecting Codes

Error-correcting codes are widely used on wireless links. There is the much lower error rate over copper wire. So error detection and retransmission is usually more efficient for dealing with the occasional error.

1. Modulo 2 arithmetic

In **modulo** 2 **arithmetic**, there are no **carries** for addition or **borrows** for subtraction, as shown in Figure 3. 1. Both addition and subtraction are identical to exclusive OR. Long **division** is carried out the same way as it is in binary except that the subtraction is done modulo 2, as above.

10011011	00110011	11110000	01010101
+11001010	+11001101	−10100110	−10101111
01010001	11111110	01010110	11111010

Figure 3. 1 Modulo 2 Arithmetic of Addition and Subtraction

2. Cyclic Redundancy Check

Another widely used encoding method is polynomial code, also known as a CRC (Cyclic Redundancy Check). **Polynomial** codes are based upon bit strings with 0 or 1 represented the polynomial **coefficients**. For example, the bit string of polynomials $x^5 + x^3 + 1$ is 101001.

When the polynomial code method is employed, the sender and receiver must agree upon a **generator polynomial**, $G(x)$, in advance. Moreover, both the highest and lowest bits of the generator must be 1. To compute the **checksum** for a m-bits frame, the frame must be longer than the polynomial $G(x)$.

The algorithm of computing the checksum is as follows.

(1) Let r be the degree of $G(x)$ and the data frame D. Append r zero bits to the low-order end of the data frame, so it contains $m+r$ bits or corresponds to $x^r D$.

(2) The bit string $x^r D$ divided by the bit string corresponding to $G(x)$ using modulo 2 divisions. The remainder R is the checksum of the frame to be transmitted, called $T(x)$.

(3) The bit string $x^r D$ minus the **remainder** R using modulo 2 subtractions. The result is the transmitted frame or check-summed frame.

Figure 3.2 illustrates the calculation process of the checksum for a data frame 101110 using the generator $G(x)=x^3+1$.

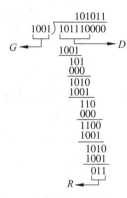

Figure 3.2   Calculation of the checksum

According to the calculation result, the transmitted frame is 101110000011.

3. Error Detection

The idea of CRC is to append a checksum to the end of the frame in such a way that the polynomial representing the transmitted frame can be divisible by $G(x)$. When the receiver gets the transmitted frame, it tries dividing it by $G(x)$. If there is a remainder, there has been a transmission error.

Notes

① It can be achieved by using exclusive OR. 这里的 it 指代前面的海明距离,海明距离可以通过异或运算获得。

② If a check bit contributes to the data bit, it may be included in the parity computation of the data bit. 这里的 it 指代 check bit 检查位。

New Words and Phrases

redundant	[ri'dʌndənt]	*adj.*	多余的,过多的;累赘的,冗长的
parity	['pærəti]	*n.*	相等;势均力敌;奇偶性
even	['i:vn]	*adj.*	平坦的;平和的;偶数的;相等的

odd	[ɔd]	*adj.*	奇数的;古怪的;零散的;剩余的
lower limit			下限;低限
theoretical	[ˌθiəˈretikl]	*adj.*	理论上的
continuously	[kənˈtinjuɒsli]	*adv.*	不断地;连续地
power	[ˈpaʊə]	*n.*	力量;力;权力;[数]幂;电力
carry	[ˈkæri]	*n.*	进位;运载
borrow	[ˈbɔrəʊ]	*v.*	借;借鉴;抄袭
division	[diˈviʒn]	*n.*	划分;除法;部门;分开
polynomial	[ˌpɔliˈnəumiəl]	*n.*	多项式
coefficient	[ˌkəʊəˈfiʃənt]	*n.*	系数
checksum	[ˈtʃeksʌm]	*n.*	检查和;校验和
remainder	[riˈmeində]	*n.*	剩余物;其余的人;[数]余数

Computer Terminologies

Hamming code	海明码
CRC(Cyclic Redundancy Check)	循环冗余校验码
error-correcting code	纠错码
error-detecting codes	检错码
codeword	码字
exclusive OR	异或
modulo 2 arithmetic	模 2 算法
generator polynomial	生成多项式

Exercises

I. Answer the questions.

1. Within Hamming code, if the 1st, 2nd, 8th check bits are wrong, then which data bit you can calculate is wrong in the frame?

2. Within Hamming code, how many check bits will you need in 1000 bits data block, and how about 1 M data block?

3. Within CRC, if the frame you want to transmit is 1101011011, and the generator polynomial is $x^4 + x + 1$, calculate the check-summed frame.

II. Fill in the blanks with these words *odd*, *checksum*, *modulo 2 arithmetic*, *Hamming code*, *codeword*, *redundant*, *division*, *CRC*

1. (   ) is error-correcting codes, and (   ) is error-detecting codes.

2. Normally, a frame consists of *m* data bits and *r* (   ) bits.

3. An *n*-bit ($n = m + r$) unit containing data and check bits is often referred to as an *n*-bit (   ).

4. Similarly, for (   ) parity schemes, the parity bit value is chosen such that there are an odd number of 1's.

5. In (   ), there are no carries for addition or borrows for subtraction.

6. Long (   ) is carried out the same way as it is in binary except that the subtraction is done modulo 2.

7. To compute the (   ) for a m-bits frame, the frame must be longer than the polynomial $G(x)$.

Extending Your Reading

Case history—Norm Abramson and ALOHANET

Norm Abramson, a PhD engineer, had a passion for surfing and an interest in packet switching. This combination of interests brought him to the University of Hawaii in 1969. Hawaii consists of many mountainous islands, making it difficult to install and operate land-based networks. When not surfing, Abramson thought about how to design a network that does packet switching over radio. The network he designed had one central host and several secondary nodes scattered over the Hawaiian Islands. The network had two channels, each using a different frequency band. For the collision inevitably occurred in the upstream channel, Abramson devised the pure ALOHA protocol. In 1970, with continued funding from APAR, Abramson connected his ALOHAnet to the APARnet. A few years after Abramson invented it, Metcalfe modified the ALOHA protocol to create the CSMA/CD protocol and the Ethernet LAN.

参考译文

差错检测与纠正

数据链路层的主要功能包括为网络层提供一个良好定义的服务接口、处理传输错误以及调整数据流。数据链路层最重要的任务是为信息通过物理层提供可靠的传输。目前,有两种已经成熟的处理错误的策略:海明码和循环冗余校验码。前者是纠错码,后者是检错码。我们将按顺序研究它们。

海明码

海明距离

一般,一帧包含 m 个数据位和 r 个冗余位。冗余位用来检测或者纠正错误。一个包含数据位和检测位的 n 位(n 等于 m 加 r)单元经常被称为 n 位码字。

给出任意两个码字,10001001 和 10110001,可以确定有多少对应位不同。此处有 3 位不同。两个码字不同的位数个数叫做海明距离。它可以通过异或运算获得。

奇偶校验

假如信息 D 要被发送,它有 d 比特位。在偶校验中,发送方只简单地增加一位作为校验位,选择其值为:使得 $d+1$ 位中 1 的总个数为偶数个。也就是说,如果在原始信息中加上一个校验位后 1 的个数为偶数,就叫做偶校验。同样地,奇校验方案就是选择校验位的值来保证 1 的个数为奇数。比如,当 1011011 以偶校验模式发送,在末尾增加一位,变成 10110111。如果是奇校验,则把 1001010 变成 10010100。

海明编码

假如一个包含 m 信息位,r 校验位的码字,可以纠正所有的单个错误。$n=m+r$,要求满足不等式 $(m+r+1) \leqslant 2^r$。给定 m,这个式子给出了用来纠正所有单一错误的校验位数的下界。

实际上,这个理论上的下界能够由海明码达到。海明码的方法如下。首先,对码字的每一位连续编号,从左边的第一个 1 比特位开始,接在它右边的第二位,等等。然后 2 的幂次位(如 1、2、4、8、16,等等)是校验位、剩下的位(如 3、5、6、7、9,等等)由数据位来填充。最后,每一个校验位都迫使某一组位(包括它自己)的奇偶值为偶数或者(奇数)。数据位数 k,重写它的值为 2 的幂次方的和。如果校验位对数据位有贡献,那么它就被包含在数据位的奇偶计算中。比如,$11=1+2+8$。使用偶校验来编码 8 位二进制数据 10101111,编码之后的值为 101001001111。

检错码

检错码广泛使用于无线网络上。铜线上有更低的误码率,所以,使用差错检测和重传能更有效地处理突发性错误。

模 2 运算

在模 2 运算中,加法中没有进位,减法中没有借位,如图 3.1 所示。加法和减法都等价于异或运算。长除法与二进制中的长除运算一样,只不过减法按模 2 运算,如前所述。

$$
\begin{array}{cccc}
10011011 & 00110011 & 11110000 & 01010101 \\
+11001010 & +11001101 & -10100110 & -10101111 \\
\hline
01010001 & 11111110 & 01010110 & 11111010
\end{array}
$$

图 3.1　模 2 加减法运算

循环冗余校验码

另外一种广泛使用的编码方式是多项式编码,也叫做循环冗余校验码。多项式编码基于多项式系数的 0 或者 1 的字符串。例如,多项式 x^5+x^3+1 的多项式编码是 101001。当使用多项式编码方法时,发送方和接收方之间必须提前对生成表达式 $G(x)$ 达成一致。更多的是,生成表达式的最高位和最低位都必须是 1。为了计算一个 m 位长的帧的校验和,帧的长度必须比生成多项式 $G(x)$ 长。

计算校验和的算法如下。

(1) r 是生成表达式 $G(x)$ 的度,数据帧为 D。数据帧的低阶增加 r 个 0 比特位,所以包含有 $m+r$ 比特位,对应的多项式为 $x^r D$。

(2) 多项式 $x^r D$ 对应的位串被 $G(x)$ 对应的位串采用模 2 除法进行整除。余数 R 就是要被传输的帧的校验和,叫做 $T(x)$。

(3) 字符串 $x^r D$ 采用模 2 减法减去余数 R。结果就是要被传输的帧或者叫做带校验和的帧。

图 3.2 表明了数据帧为 101110,生成式为 $G(x)=x^3+1$ 的校验和的计算过程。根据计

算的结果，传输的帧为 101110000011。

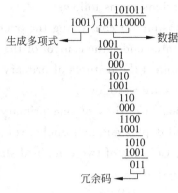

图 3.2　计算校验和

错误检测

循环冗余校验码的思想是在帧的末端增加了一个校验和，这样表达传输的帧的多项式能被生成表达式 $G(x)$ 除。当接收者获得发送来的帧，用它去除 $G(x)$，如果有余数，就说明传输出错。

Section B   Example Data Link Protocols

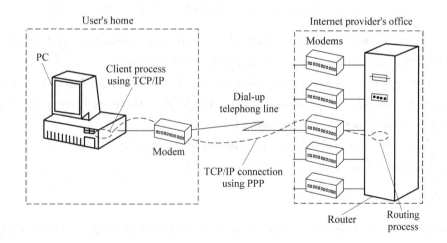

I. Introduction

The most important **data link control protocol** is **HDLC**（High Data Link Control），and the second one，**PPP**（Point-to-Point Protocol），is also the data link protocol used to connect home computers to the Internet.

II. HDLC

1. Basic concepts

HDLC is bit oriented and uses bit **stuffing** for data **transparency**. It defines three types of stations, two link configurations, and three data transfer modes of operation to satisfy a variety of applications. The stations are as follows.

- **Primary station**: Responsible for controlling the operation of the link.
- **Secondary station**: Operates under the control of the primary station.
- **Combined station**: Combined the features of primary and secondary.

The two link configurations are as follows.

- **Unbalanced configuration**: Consists of one primary and one or more secondary stations, and supports both full-duplex and half-duplex transmission.
- **Balanced configuration**: Consists of two combined stations, and supports both full-duplex and half-duplex transmission.

The three transfer modes are as follows.

- **Normal response mode (NRM)**: Used with an unbalanced configuration.
- **Asynchronous balanced mode (ABM)**: Used with a balanced configuration.
- **Asynchronous response mode (ARM)**: Used with an unbalanced configuration.

2. The frame structure

The frame structure of HDLC is shown in Figure 3.3.

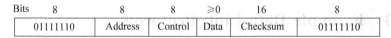

Figure 3.3　Frame format for HDLC

The *Address* field is used to identify one of the terminals, and sometimes to distinguish commands from responses for point-to-point lines. ①

The *Control* field is used for sequence numbers, acknowledgements, and other purposes. ② According to the contents of the control field, there are three kinds of frames: Information, **Supervisory**, and **Unnumbered**.

The *Data* field may contain any information with arbitrarily long.

The *Checksum* field is a cyclic redundancy code.

III. PPP

The point-to-point protocol (PPP) is used in the data link layer of the Internet. It has three features: a framing method, a link control protocol (LCP), and network Control Protocol (NCP). The LCP is responsible for bringing lines up, testing them, negotiating options, and bringing them down again gracefully when they are no longer needed. ③ The NCP provides a way to negotiate network-layer options. The major difference between PPP and HDLC is that PPP is character oriented rather than **bit oriented**.

The PPP frame format is shown in Figure 3.4.

All PPP frames begin with 01111110, which is byte stuffed if it occurs within the **payload** field.

The *Address* field is set to the binary value 11111111 to indicate that all stations are

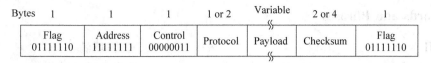

Figure 3.4   Frame format for PPP

to accept the frame.

The *Control* field has the default value of 00000011, which indicates an unnumbered frame.

The *Protocol* field is to tell what kind of packet is in the *Payload* field.

The *Payload* field is variable length, up to some negotiated maximum.

The *Checksum* field is normally 2 bytes, but a 4-byte checksum can be negotiated.

In summary, PPP is suitable for use over modems, SONET, and other physical layers. It supports error detection, option negotiation, header compression, and so on. Figure 3.5 shows the phases that a line goes through when it is brought up, used, and taken down again.

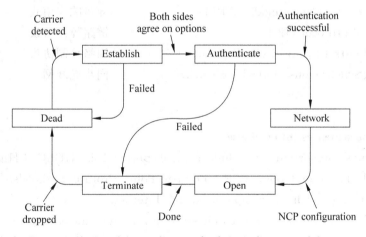

Figure 3.5   Simple state diagram for bring a line up and down

Notes

① The *Address* field is used to identify one of the terminals, and sometimes to distinguish commands from responses for point-to-point lines. 这里 is used to 翻译成"被用来"后面接动词不定式。

② The *Control* field is used for sequence numbers, acknowledgements, and other purposes. 这里 is used for 翻译成"用于"或者"用来"。

③ The LCP is responsible for bringing lines up, testing them, negotiating options, and bringing them down again gracefully when they are no longer needed. 这里 is responsible for 解释成"负责",后面接名词,或者动词的-ing 形式。

New Words and Phrases

stuff	[stʌf]	vt.	塞满；填满
transparency	[træns'pærənsi]	n.	透明度；幻灯片
supervisory	[ˌsjuːpə'vaizəri]	adj.	管理的；监控的
unnumbered	[ʌn'nʌmbəd]	adj.	未编号的；数不清的；无数的
bit oriented			面向比特的
payload	['peiləʊd]	n.	有效载重；负载

Computer Terminologies

data link control protocol	数据链路控制协议
HDLC（High Data Link Control）	高级数据链路控制协议
PPP（Point-to-Point Protocol）	点对点协议
Normal response mode（NRM）	正常响应模式
Asynchronous balanced mode（ABM）	异步平衡模式
Asynchronous response mode（ARM）	异步响应模式
link control protocol（LCP）	链路控制协议
network Control Protocol（NCP）	网络控制协议
SONET（Synchronous Optical Network）	同步光纤网

Exercises

I. Translate the sentences into Chinese.

1. The most important data link control protocol is HDLC (High Data Link Control)，and the second one，PPP (Point-to-Point Protocol)，is also the data link protocol used to connect home computers to the Internet.

2. HDLC is bit oriented and uses bit stuffing for data transparency.

3. The point-to-point protocol (PPP) is used in the data link layer of the Internet. It has three features：a framing method，a link control protocol (LCP)，and network Control Protocol (NCP).

4. The major difference between PPP and HDLC is that PPP is character oriented rather than bit oriented.

5. In summary，PPP is suitable for use over modems，SONET，and other physical layers.

II. Answer the questions.

1. If you are at home and you want to connect the Internet，then which protocol you need to install HDLC or PPP?

2. What are the differences between bit oriented and character oriented?

Extending Your Reading

Principles in practice—Keeping the layers independent

There are several reasons why nodes have MAC addresses in addition to network-layer addressed. First, LANs are designed for arbitrary network-layer protocols, not just for IP and the Internet. If adapters were assigned IP addresses rather than "neutral" MAC addresses, then adapters would not easily be able to support other network-layer protocols. Second, if adapters were to use network-layer addresses instead of MAC addresses, the network-layer address would have to be stored in the adapter RAM and reconfigured every time the adapter was moved (or power up). In summary, in order for the layers to be largely independent building blocks in the network architecture, many layers need to have their own addressing scheme. Generally, three types of addresses are used in hosts: host name for the application layer, IP address for the network layer, and MAC address for the data link layer.

参考译文

数据链路协议举例

最重要的数据链路控制协议是 HDLC(高级数据链路控制协议)还有 PPP(点对点协议),它也是家庭计算机用来接入因特网的数据链路协议。

HDLC

基本概念

HDLC 是一个面向比特的协议,它使用比特填充来保证数据透明。它定义了三种类型的基站、两种链路配置、三种操作数据传输模式用来满足应用变化。基站定义如下所示。

- 主站:负责控制链路操作。
- 次站:在主站控制下操作。
- 联合站:结合了主站和次站的特点。

两种链路配置如下。

- 非平衡配置:包含一个主站,一个或者多个次站,支持全双工和半双工传输。
- 平衡配置:包含两个联合站,支持全双工和半双工传输。

三种传输模式如下。

- 正常响应模式:与非平衡配置一起使用。
- 异步平衡模式:与平衡配置一起使用。
- 异步响应模式:与非平衡配置一起使用。

帧结构

HDLC 的帧结构如图 3.3 所示。

地址字段用来代表目的地址,有时用来区分点对点链路的应答命令。

控制字段用来表示序列号、确认以及其他目的。根据控制字段的内容,有三种类型的

位	8	8	8	≥0	16	8
	01111110	地址	控制	数据	校验和	01111110

图 3.3　HDLC 帧格式

帧：信息帧、监督帧和非序号帧。

数据字段包含任意长的信息。

校验字段保存的是循环冗余校验码。

PPP

点对点协议用在因特网的数据链路层。它有三个性质：成帧方法、链路控制协议以及网络控制协议。链路控制协议负责启动线路、测试线路、协商参数，以及当线路不再需要时温和地中断连接。网络控制协议提供一种方法协议网络层选项。PPP 和 HDLC 协议的主要区别是：一个是面向比特，另一个是面向字节。

PPP 的帧格式如图 3.4 所示。

字节	1	1	1	1 or 2	可变长度	2 or 4	1
	标志 01111110	地址 11111111	控制 00000011	协议	净荷	校验和	标志 01111110

图 3.4　PPP 帧格式

所有的 PPP 帧是以 01111110 开始，如果它出现在负载字段中，则需要以字节填充。

地址字段设置二进制值，11111111 表示所有的站都要接受此帧。

控制字段的默认值是 00000011，表明是一个无序号帧。

协议字段是说明在负载字段存放的是什么种类的包。

负载字段是可变长度，最大达到协商的最大值。

校验和字段一般是 2 字节，但是也可以协议达到 4 字节。

总之，PPP 适合于调制解调器、同步光纤网和其他的物理层。它支持错误检测、选项协商、头压缩等。图 3.5 显示了一个线路建立连接、使用、中断的步骤。

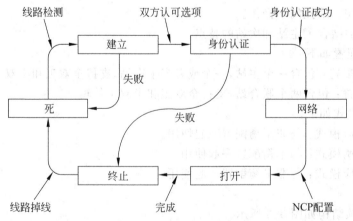

图 3.5　从线路启动到关闭的简单状态图

Section C   Ethernet and Wireless LANs

I. Introduction

The LAN is widely used for a variety of applications. One of its features is using broadcast channels. In any broadcast network, the key issue is how to determine who gets to use the channel when there is competition for it, and the corresponding protocols belong to **multiple access** protocols. Among them, **CSMA/CD** is an important protocol widely used in the **Ethernet**.

II. CSMA/CD

1. The operating principle of CSMA/CD

The operating principle of CSMA/CD (Carrier Sense Multiple Access with Collision Detection) is as follows. Firstly, when a station wants to transmit, it **senses** the channel. If the channel is **idle**, the station sends the data immediately. If the channel is busy, it continues to sense the channel until the channel is idle. Secondly, stations detect the **collision**. If two stations sense the channel to be idle and begin transmitting simultaneously, the collision happens and the transmission stops **abruptly** as soon as the collision is detected by any station. Thirdly, if a collision occurs, the colliding stations wait a random time, using the Ethernet **binary exponential back-off algorithm**, and then try again later.

The model for CSMA/CD consists of alternating **contention** and transmission periods, with idle periods occurring when all stations are quiet. [1] How long will it take stations to realize that there has been a collision? From Figure 3.6, we can see that τ is the end-to-end delay or the worst-case **round-trip** propagation time. So, it will take 2τ to realize the collision occurring.

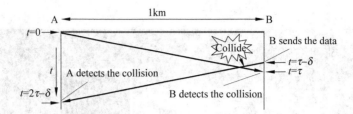

Figure 3.6   The round-trip propagation time is 2τ

2. The binary exponential back-off algorithm

After a collision, time is divided into **discrete slots** whose length is equal to 2τ. To **accommodate** the longest path allowed by Ethernet with 10Mbps, the slot time has been set to 51.2μsec. Ethernet requires that valid frames must be at least 64bytes long, from destination address to checksum.

After the first collision, each station waits either 0 or 1 slot times before trying again. After the second collision, each one picks either 0, 1, 2, or 3 at random and waits that number of slot times. Assume that the number of collision is i. In general, when the value of i is lower than 10, the waiting time is set to i slot times. If the value of i is larger than or equal to 10 but lower than 16, the waiting time is 1023 slot times. After 16 collisions, the controller reports failure back to the higher layers.

III. Ethernet

Generally, the name "Ethernet" refers to the cable (the ether). So, we start with the Ethernet cables, and then study the **Manchester Encoding** and the Ethernet **MAC** sub-layer protocol.

1. Ethernet cables

Four types of cabling commonly used is shown in Figure 3.7. The **notation** 10Base5 means that it operates at 10Mbps, uses base-band signaling, and can support **segments** of up to 500 meters. The first number is the speed in Mbps. The word "Base" indicates **base-band** transmission.

Name	Cable	Max.seg.	Nodes/seg.	Advantages
10Base5	Thick coax	500m	100	Original cable;now obsolete
10Base2	Thin coax	185m	30	No hub needed
10Base-T	Twisted pair	100m	1024	Cheapest system
10Base-F	Fiber optics	2000m	1024	Best between buildings

Figure 3.7   Kinds of Ethernet cable

2. Manchester Encoding

There are two encoding approaches for users to **unambiguously** determine the start, end, or middle of each bit without reference to an external clock. They are Manchester encoding and differential Manchester encoding. With Manchester encoding, each bit period is divided into two equal **intervals**. A binary 1bit is sent by having the voltage set high during the first interval and low in the second one. A binary 0 is just the reverse: first low and then high. This scheme ensures that every bit period has a **transition** in the middle, making it easy for the receiver to **synchronize** with the sender. [2]

Differential Manchester encoding is a variation of basic Manchester encoding. In it, a 1bit is indicated by the absence of a transition at the start of the interval. A 0bit is indicated by the presence of a transition at the start of the interval, as shown in Figure 3.8. The differential scheme requires more complex equipment but offers better noise **immunity**. All Ethernet systems use Manchester encoding due to its simplicity.

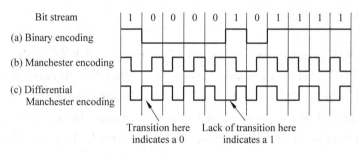

Figure 3.8   Manchester encoding

3. The Ethernet MAC sub-layer protocol

There are two kinds of frame structure of the Ethernet: **DIX Ethernet V2**, **IEEE** 802.3, as shown in Figure 3.9.

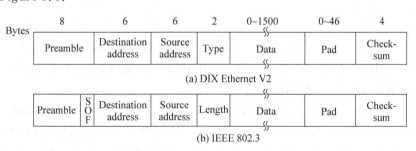

Figure 3.9   Frame formats

The *Type* field tells the receiver what to do with the frame. If its value is larger than or equal to 0600H, it indicates the types of the protocol used in its upper layer, corresponding to the DIX Ethernet. [3] If its value is lower than 0600H, it is the length of the *data* field, corresponding to IEEE 802.3.

4. High-speed Ethernet

Except for the Ethernet, there are other Ethernets with higher speed, such as **Switched Ethernet**, **Fast Ethernet**, **Gigabit Ethernet**.

5. Logic link control

Logical Link Control (LLC) hides the differences between the various kinds of IEEE 802 networks by providing a single format and interface to the network layer.

In short, Ethernet is simple and flexible.

IV. Wireless LANs

Wireless LANs can operate in one of two configurations: with a base station or without a base station. The IEEE 802.11 standard is used for them.

In IEEE 802.11, the MAC sub-layer determines how the channel is allocated, that is, who gets to transmit next. Above it is the LLC sub-layer, which hides the differences between the different IEEE 802 variants and make them indistinguishable as far as the network layer is concerned.

CSMA/CA

The IEEE 802.11 supports two modes of operation: DCF (Distributed Coordination Function) and PCF (Point Coordination Function). When DCF is employed, IEEE 802.11 uses a protocol called CSMA/CA (CSMA with Collision Avoidance). CSMA/CA uses both physical channel sensing and virtual channel sensing. In physical channel sensing, when a station wants to transmit, it senses the channel. If it is idle, it just starts transmitting. It does not sense the channel while transmitting but **emits** its entire frame. If the channel is busy, the sender **defers** until it goes idle and then starts transmitting. If a collision occurs, the colliding stations wait a random time, using the Ethernet binary exponential back-off algorithm, and then try again later.

Notes

① The model for CSMA/CD consists of alternation contention and transmission periods, with idle periods occurring when all stations are quiet. 在这句话中，occurring when all stations are quiet 修饰前面的 idle periods。

② This scheme ensures that every bit period has a transition in the middle, making it easy for the receiver to synchronize with the sender. 这里的 it 指代前面的 every bit period。

③ If its value is larger than or equal to 0600H, it indicates the types of the protocol used in its upper layer, corresponding to the DIX Ethernet. 这里的 it 指代前面的 its value，意思是此字段的值代表上层使用的协议的类型，本句中的第二个 its upper layer 代表"本层的上层"。

New Words and Phrases

sense	[sens]	v.	感觉；意识到；理解；检测
idle	[ˈaidl]	adj.	无目的；无聊的；懒惰的；闲散的
collision	[kəˈliʒn]	n.	碰撞；冲突
abruptly	[əˈbrʌptli]	adv.	突然地；莽撞地；陡峭地；不连贯地

contention	[kən'tenʃn]	*n.*	争论；争辩；争夺；论点
round-trip			来回旅行；双程旅行
discrete	[di'skri:t]	*adj.*	不连续的；分离的
slot	[slɔt]	*n.*	狭缝；槽；投币口；时间段；职位
accommodate	[ə'kɔmədeit]	*vt.*	供给住宿；使适应；容纳；提供
notation	[nəʊ'teiʃn]	*n.*	记号；表示法；注释；记法
segment	['segmənt]	*n.*	部分；弓形；瓣；段；节
unambiguously	[ˌʌnæm'bigjuəsli]	*adv.*	不含糊的；清楚的
interval	['intəvəl]	*n.*	间隔；休息时间；(数学)区间
transition	[træn'ziʃn]	*n.*	转变；过渡
synchronize	['siŋkrənaiz]	*vt.*	使同步；使同时发生
immunity	[i'mju:nəti]	*n.*	免疫；免疫性；免除；豁免
emit	[i'mit]	*vt.*	发出，发射；放射；吐露
defer	[di'fɛ:]	*v.*	推迟；延期；使延期入伍

Computer Terminologies

multiple access	多点接入
CSMA/CD(Carrier Sense Multiple Access with Collision Detection)	带冲突检测载波监听多路访问
Ethernet	以太网(局域网)
binary exponential back-off algorithm	二进制指数退避算法
Manchester Encoding	曼彻斯特编码
MAC(Medium Access Control)	介质访问控制
base-band	基带
Differential Manchester encoding	差分曼彻斯特编码
DIX Ethernet V2	DIX 第二代以太网
Switched Ethernet	交换式以太网
Fast Ethernet	快速以太网
Gigabit Ethernet	千兆以太网
Logical Link Control (LLC)	逻辑链路控制
DCF(Distributed Coordination Function)	分布式协调功能
PCF(Point Coordination Function)	点协调功能
CSMA/CA (CSMA with Collision Avoidance)	带冲突避免载波监听多路访问

Exercises

I. Answer the questions.

1. What does *carrier sense multiple access* mean?

2. Within CSMA/CD，How long will it take stations to realize that there has been a collision?

3. What does the notation 10Base-T mean?

4. Describe the differences between the Manchester Encoding and the Differential Manchester encoding?

5. What are the functions of MAC and LLC?

6. What does CSMA/CA mean?

II. **Fill in the blanks with these words** *senses，segments，binary exponential back-off algorithm，collision，abruptly，notation，base-band，idle.*

1. The operating principle of CSMA/CD (Carrier Sense Multiple Access with Collision Detection) is as follows. Firstly, when a station wants to transmit, it (   ) the channel. If the channel is (   ), the station sends the data immediately. If the channel is busy, it continues to sense the channel until the channel is idle. Secondly, stations detect the (   ). If two stations sense the channel to be idle and begin transmitting simultaneously, the collision happens and the transmission stops (   ) as soon as the collision is detected by any station. Thirdly, if a collision occurs, the colliding stations wait a random time, using the Ethernet (   ), and then try again later.

2. The (   ) 10Base5 means that it operates at 10Mbps, uses base-band signaling, and can support (   ) of up to 500 meters. The first number is the speed in Mbps. The word "Base" indicates (   ) transmission.

Extending Your Reading

Case history—Bob Metcalfe and Ethernet

As a PhD student at Harvard University in the early 1970s, Bob Metcalfe worked on the ARPAnet at MIT. During his studies, he also became exposed to Abramson's work on ALOHA and random access protocols. After completing his PhD, Metcalfe saw the need to network these computers in an inexpensive manner. So, armed with his knowledge about ARPAnet, ALOHAnet and random access protocols, Metcalfe—along with colleague David Boggs—invented Ethernet.

Metcalfe and Boggs's original Ethernet ran at 2.94Mbps and link up to 256hosts separated by up to one mile. In 1979, Metcalfe formed his own company, 3Com, which developed and commercialized networking technology, including Ethernet technology. In particular, 3Com developed and marketed Ethernet cards in the early 1980 for the immensely popular IBM PCs.

参考译文

以太网和无线局域网

局域网广泛使用于各种应用。它的特点之一就是使用广播通道。在任何的广播网络中最关键的问题是当竞争产生时，如何决定谁使用信道，而相应使用的协议则属于多点接入协议。在这些协议中间,CSMA/CD(带冲突检测载波监听多路访问)是一个非常重要的广泛用于以太网的协议。

CSMA/CD

CSMA/CD 的操作原理

CSMA/CD 的操作原理如下。首先,当一个站点想要传输信息时,它侦听信道。如果信道空闲,那么站点立即发送数据。如果信道繁忙,则继续侦听信道直到信道空闲。接着,站点检测冲突。如果两个站点发现信道是空闲的,都开始同时发送数据,冲突便会产生,一旦冲突被任何站点检测到,传输将尽可能快地被突然终止。最后,如果冲突发生,冲突的站点等待一段用以太网二进制指数退避算法获得的随机时间,接着继续侦听。

CSMA/CD 模型包含了轮换、竞争、传输时间以及当所有站点都空闲时的闲散时间。一个站点需要多长时间才认识到冲突已经发生了? 从图 3.6 中,我们可以知道 τ 是端到端的延迟或者说是最坏情况下来回传播时间。所以,需要 2τ 的时间认识到冲突发生。

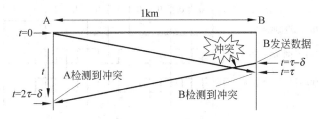

图 3.6　来回传输时延为 2τ

二进制指数退避算法

冲突发生之后,时间被划分成离散的时隙,长度等于 2τ。为了适应10Mbps的以太网所允许的最长路径,时隙长度设置为 $51.2\mu s$。以太网要求合法帧从目的地址到校验和的长度至少为 64 字节长。

在第一次冲突发生之后,每一个站点等待 0 个或者 1 个时隙时间再接着侦听。在第二次冲突发生之后,每一个站点随机选择 0、1、2 或者 3 个时隙时间。假如是第 i 次发生冲突,一般来说,当 i 的值小于 10,等待时间设置为 i 个时隙时间。如果 i 的值大于或者等于 10 而小于 16,等待时间为 1023 个时隙时间。在 16 次冲突之后,控制器向高层汇报失败。

以太网

一般,名字"以太网"指的是电缆(以太)。因此,我们从以太电缆开始,然后研究曼彻斯特编码和以太 MAC(介质访问控制)子层协议。

以太网电缆

图 3.7 显示了四种常用的电缆类型。符号 10Base5 意思是指它以 10Mbps 的速度运行,使用基带信号,可以支持 500m 范围。第一个数字表示单位为 Mbps 的速度。单词"Base"指的是基带传输。

曼彻斯特编码

有两种编码方式用户可以清楚地分辨每一比特的开始、结束、中间,而不需要一个外部时钟,它们是曼彻斯特编码和差分曼彻斯特编码。对于曼彻斯特编码,每一比特长度分成两

名称	线缆	最大段大小	节点数/段	优点
10Base5	粗同轴电缆	500m	100	早期电缆，现已废弃
10Base2	细同轴电缆	185m	30	不需要集线器
10Base-T	双绞线	100m	1024	最便宜的系统
10Base-F	光纤	2000m	1024	最适合在楼栋间使用

图 3.7　以太网电缆类型

份等长的区间。二进制 1 在前半个时间片以高电平发送，在后半个时间片以低电平发送。二进制 0 刚好相反：首先低电平然后再高电平。这种方案确保了每个比特周期在其中间点都有电平转换，这使得发送者和接收者之间容易同步。

差分曼彻斯特编码是一个基本曼彻斯特编码的变形。1 比特在周期开始时电压不产生变换。0 比特在周期开始时电压变换，如图 3.8 所示。差分编码模式要求更复杂的设备，但是提供了更好的抗噪能力。因为曼彻斯特编码的简单性，所有的以太网都使用它。

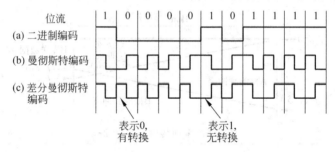

图 3.8　曼彻斯特编码

以太网的介质访问控制子层协议

有两种类型的以太网帧结构：DIX Ethernet V2 和 IEEE 802.3，如图 3.9 所示。

图 3.9　帧格式

Type 字段告诉接收者如何处理帧。如果它的值大于或等于 0600H，表明是上层使用的协议，这时是 DIX Ethernet 帧。如果它的值小于 0600H，它就是指与 IEEE 802.3 相对应的 data 字段的长度。

高速以太网

除了以太网，还有其他更高速的以太网，如交换式以太网、快速以太网、千兆以太网。

逻辑链路控制

逻辑链路控制通过向网络层提供一个唯一的格式和接口的方式隐藏各种 IEEE 802 网

络的不同点。

　　总之,以太网简单灵活。

无线局域网

　　无线局域网以两种配置方式中的一种操作：有基站或者无基站。使用 IEEE 802.11 标准。

　　在 IEEE 802.11 中,介质访问控制(MAC)子层决定信道如何分配,也就是说,谁下一个传输。在 MAC 之上是逻辑链路控制层,它隐藏了各种 IEEE 802 网络的不同,使得网络层不区分它们。

CSMA/CA

　　IEEE 802.11 支持两种操作模式：DCF(分布式协调功能)、PCF(点协调功能)。当采用分布式协调功能时,IEEE 802.11 采用一个叫做 CSMA/CA(带冲突避免载波多路存取)的协议。CSMA/CA 既使用物理信道侦听又使用虚拟信道侦听。在物理信道侦听中,当一个站点要发送信息,它先侦听信道。如果信道空闲,站点开始发送信息。当发送信息时它不再侦听信道,但是发出它的整个帧。如果信道繁忙,发送者推迟发送直到信道空闲再开始传输数据。如果冲突发生,冲突的站点等待一段使用以太网的二进制指数退避算法获得的随机时间,接着再侦听。

Section D　Network Interconnection Devices

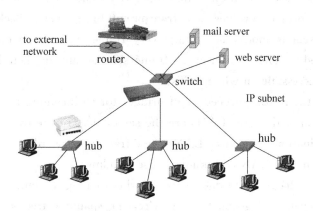

I. Introduction

　　There are a variety of ways to get frames from one cable to another. These network devices are **repeaters，hubs，bridges，switches，routers**，and so on. Repeaters and hubs operate in the physical layer. LANs can be connected by bridges or switches，which operate in the data link layer. [①] However，routers do routing by examining the addresses in packets and operate in the network layer. Now we mainly look at hubs，bridges，switches and routers in turn.

II. Hubs

Generally, the hub is used in a star-topology LAN and it is the center of the star layout. Each station is connected to the hub by a UTP or optical fiber. The hub acts as a repeater: when a single station transmits, the hub repeats the signal on the outgoing line to each station. However, this scheme is physically a star. A transmission from one station is received by all other stations. If two or more stations transmit at the same time, there will be a collision. If the total data rate of the hub connecting 5 stations is 10Mbps in the LAN, the data rate of each station is 2Mbps.

III. Bridges

The bridge is the simple means of interconnecting similar LANs that use identical protocols in the physical and link layer. [2] They are capable of mapping one MAC format to another.

When the bridges are first **plugged in**, all the hash tables are empty. There are two approaches to create the hash tables: **flooding algorithm** and **backward learning**. The flooding algorithm operates as follows: every incoming frame for an unknown destination is output on all the LANs to which the bridge is connected except the one it arrived on. [3] As time goes on, the bridges learn where destinations are. Once a destination is known, frames destined for it are put on only the proper LAN and are not flooded. [4]

The simplest form of bridges is a **transparent** bridge using backward learning. It operates in promiscuous mode, accepting every frame transmitted on all the LANs to which it is attached[5]. They watch every frame sent on any of their LANs and can tell which machine is **accessible** on which LAN.

In summary, the routing procedure of bridges for an incoming frame is as follows.

- If destination and source LANs are the same, discard the frame.
- If the destination and source LANs are different, forward the frame.
- If the destination LAN is unknown, use flooding.

However, once **loops** of bridges exist in the topology, some additional problems occur. A frame's cycle will go on forever. Creating **spanning tree** is the best method to solve this problem. Once the bridges have agreed on the spanning tree, all forwarding between LANs has a unique path from each source to each destination, and loops are impossible.

IV. Switches

The switch operates in the data link layer and is often used to connect individual computers, as shown in Figure 3.10. Each line card of switches provides buffer space for frames arriving on its ports, so it never loses

Figure 3.10　The switch device

frames to collisions. There are two types of switches available as commercial products: **cut-through switches** and **store-and-forward switches**.

The store-and-forward switch accepts a frame from an input line, buffers it briefly and routes it to the appropriate output line. The cut-through switch begins repeating the incoming frame onto the appropriate output line as soon as it gets the destination MAC address appearing in the MAC frame. The cut-through switch yields the highest possible throughput but at some risk of propagating bad frames. The store-and-forward switch involves a delay between sender and receiver but boosts the overall integrity of the network.

V. Routers

The router is a network interconnecting device operating in the network layer. It has **multi-input**s and multi-outputs, whose main task is to **forward** packets. The inner architecture of the router is shown in Figure 3.11. It consists of four components: input ports, switching **fabric**, output ports and routing processor. The routing processor executes the routing protocols or algorithms, maintains the routing tables, and performs network management functions. The switching fabric connects the router's input ports to its output ports and performs packet forwarding.

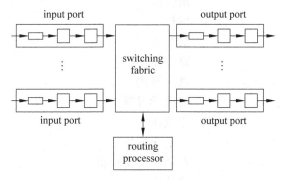

Figure 3.11   Router architecture

Notes

① LANs can be connected by bridges or switches, which operate in the data link layer. 这里的 which 引导定语从句,它指代前面的 bridges 或者 switches,网桥或者交换机是工作在数据链路层。

② The bridge is the simple means of interconnecting similar LANs that use identical protocols in the physical and link layer. 这里的 that 引导定语从句,指代前面的 similar LANs,在从句中做主语,意思是"类似的局域网在物理层和链路层使用同样的协议"。

③ The flooding algorithm operates as follows: every incoming frame for an unknown destination is output on all the LANs to which the bridge is connected except the one it arrived on. 这里的 which 引导定语从句,指代连接在网桥上的所有局域网。

④ As time goes on, the bridges learn where destinations are. Once a destination is known, frames destined for it are put on only the proper LAN and are not flooded. 这里的 it 指代 destination，后面的 are not flooded 的主语是 frames destined for it。

⑤ It operates in promiscuous mode, accepting every frame transmitted on all the LANs to which it is attached. 在这句话中，accepting 的主语是 it，整个后半句 accepting every frame transmitted on all the LANs to which it is attached 修饰主语 it。which 指 LANs，it is attached 中的 it 指的是主语 bridge。

New Words and Phrases

plugged in			给……接通电源；连接
transparent	[træns'pɛərənt]	adj.	透明的；明显的；清晰的
accessible	[ək'sesəbl]	adj.	可得到的；易接近的；可进入的
loop	[luːp]	n.	环；圈；回路；环形线路
forward	['fɔːwəd]	v.	促进；转交；发送
fabric	['fæbrik]	n.	结构；织物；构造

Computer Terminologies

Repeater	中继器
Hub	集线器
Bridge	网桥
Switch	交换机
Router	路由器
flooding algorithm	洪泛算法
backward learning	逆向学习算法
spanning tree	生成树
cut-through switch	直通交换机
store-and-forward switch	存储转发交换机
multi-inputs	多输入

Exercises

I. Answer the questions.

1. Which interconnection devices do they work in data link layer and how about network layer interconnection devices?

2. Which interconnection devices are they often used in LAN?

3. Can you list the interconnection devices producer in China and list them?

4. Describe the flooding algorithm.

II. Fill in the blanks with these words *store-and-forward switches*, *hub*, *cut-through switches*, *flooding algorithm*, *transparent*, *forward*, *backward learning*, *interconnecting*.

1. The (   ) acts as a repeater: when a single station transmits, the hub repeats the signal on the outgoing line to each station.

2. When the bridges are first plugged in，all the hash tables are empty. There are two approaches to create the hash tables：(　　) and (　　).

3. The simplest form of bridges is a (　　) bridge using backward learning.

4. There are two types of switches available as commercial products：(　　) and (　　).

5. The router is a network (　　) device operating in the network layer.

6. It has multi-inputs and multi-outputs，whose main task is to (　　) packets.

Extending Your Reading

Impacts technology having on learning in the future

Eventually，almost all human knowledge will be accessible through the Internet，which will be the most powerful tool for learning. This vast knowledge base will have the potential of leveling the playing field for students all over the world. For example，motivated students in any country will be able to access the best class Web sites，multimedia lectures，and teaching materials. The Internet will transcend all geographic barriers to learning.

参考译文

网络互连设备

从线路的一端到另一端有各种各样的方式获得帧。这些网络设备是中继器、集线器、网桥、交换机等。中继器和集线器工作在物理层。局域网可以由网桥和交换机互连,这些设备工作在数据链路层。然而,路由器通过检查包中地址的方式路由,它工作在网络层。现在依次来学习集线器、网桥、交换机和路由器。

集线器

一般地,集线器用在星状拓扑局域网中,它是星状拓扑的中心。每个站点通过双绞线或者光纤连接到集线器。当单一站点发送数据时,集线器扮演中继器的角色,它将信号重复发送到连接每一个站点的外部线路上。然而,这是物理上的星状模式。一个站点发送,其他所有站点接收。如果两个或者多个站点同时发送,则存在冲突。也就是说,如果在一个局域网中,一个连接 5 个站点的集线器的速率是 10Mbps,那么每一个站点的速率就是 2Mbps。

网桥

网桥是连接同类型局域网的一种简单方式,这些局域网在物理层和数据链路层使用同样的协议。它们可以实现从一个局域网到另一个局域网的 MAC 地址映射。

当网桥第一次被插上去的时候,所有的哈希表都是空的。有两种创建哈希表的方法:洪泛法和反向学习法。洪泛法的操作原理如下:每一个发送来的帧,对于目的站点不清楚的,被发送到网桥连接到的所有除了它到达过的局域网。随着时间推移,网桥学习到目的地址。一旦知道了目的地址,发往它的目标帧被放到合适的局域网而不被洪泛。

最简单的网桥是采用反向学习的透明网桥。它工作在混杂模式,接收每一个连接到它上面的局域网发送来的帧。它们监视局域网发送的每一个帧,并能指出哪一个局域网的哪一台机器是可以到达的。

总之,接收发送来的帧的路由过程如下:

- 如果目的局域网和源局域网是相同的,则丢弃此帧。
- 如果目的局域网和源局域网不相同,则转发此帧。
- 如果不知道目的局域网,则采用洪泛法。

虽然如此,一旦在拓扑结构中存在网桥回路,一些额外的问题便产生了。帧将一直周期性地循环下去。创建生成树是解决这个问题的最好方法。一旦网桥同意生成树算法,所有的局域网之间的转发只有一个从源站点到目的站点的唯一路径,不可能产生循环。

交换机

交换机工作在数据链路层,经常用来连接单个的计算机,如图 3.10 所示。交换机的每个线路卡为每一个到达其端口的帧提供了缓存区间,因此它不会丢掉发生冲突的帧。有两种商用的交换机:直通交换机和存储-转发交换机。

存储-转发交换机接收输入线路发送来的帧,短暂缓存,并路由到相应的输出线路。直通交换机一旦获得出现

图 3.10   交换机设备

在 MAC 帧上的目的 MAC 地址,就开始将到来的帧重复发送帧到相应的输出线路上。直通交换机可达到最高可能的吞吐量,但是存在传播坏帧的风险。存储转发交换机在发送方和接收方之间有一个延迟,但是加强了网络整体的完整性。

路由器

路由器是工作在网络层的网络互连设备。它有多输入、多输出,其主要任务是转发包。路由器的结构如图 3.11 所示。它包含四个部件:输入端口、交换结构、输出端口、路由处理器。路由处理器执行路由协议或者算法,维持一个路由表,执行网络管理功能。交换结构连接路由器的输入端口到输出端口,并执行包转发。

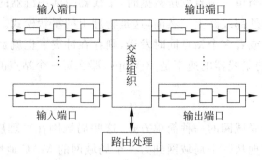

图 3.11   路由器结构

Unit 4　The Network Layer

Section A　Routing Algorithms

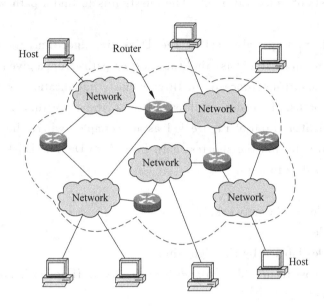

I. Introduction

The network layer is concerned with getting packets from the source all the way to the destination. Routing packets from the source to the destination is its main job. The network layer also provides either **virtual circuit** or **datagram services** to the transport layer. In virtual-circuit subnets, a routing decision is made when the virtual circuit is set up. If connectionless service is offered, no advance setup is needed.

To achieve these goals, the network layer must know about the topology of the communication subnet and choose appropriate paths through it. The routing algorithm is responsible for deciding which output line an incoming packet should be transmitted on. [1]

II. Categories of routing algorithms

Routing algorithms can be grouped into two major classes: **non-adaptive** and **adaptive**. Non-adaptive algorithms, also called **static routing**, do not make decision based on measurements or estimates of the current traffic and topology. Instead, the choice of the route is computed in advance. Examples of static routing commonly used are **shortest path routing**, and **flooding**. In contrast, adaptive algorithms change their routing decisions to reflect changes in the topology, and usually the traffic as well. It is also called dynamic routing, such as **distance vector routing**, **link state routing**.

III. Shortest path routing

Before studying the shortest path algorithm, we state the problem simply as follows:

Given a network of nodes connected by **bidirectional** links, where each link has a cost associated with it in each direction.[②] The cost of a path between two nodes is defined as the sum of the costs of links traversed. The question is to find a path with the least cost for each pair of nodes.

Shortest path routing, also called the Dijskstra algorithm, is a static routing. Dijskstra algorithm can be stated as: find the shortest paths from a given source node to all other nodes. The algorithm proceeds in three stages: initialization, get next node, and update least-cost paths. In order to illustrate how the algorithm works, we take an undirected and **weighted** graph of Figure 4.1 as an example, where the weights represent distance. The goal is to find the shortest path from A to D. The Dijskstra algorithm can be formally described as follows.

Definition:

N—set of nodes in the network.

s—source node.

T—set of nodes labeled by the algorithm.

$w(i,j)$—link cost from node i to node j. $w(i,i)=0$. If node i is not **adjacent** to node j directly, $w(i,j)=\infty$.

$L(n)$—cost of the least-cost path from node s to node n known currently according to the algorithm.

(1) **Initialization.** $T=\{s\}$, $L(n)=w(s,n)$.

(2) **Get next node.** Find x that is satisfied with $x\notin T$ and $L(x)=\min\limits_{j\notin T}L(j)$. Add x to T. If $T=N$, stop, else go step (3).

(3) **Update least-cost paths.** $L(n)=\min[L(n),L(x)+w(x,n)]$ for all $n\notin T$. Go step (2).

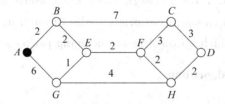

Figure 4.1   The undirected and weighted graph

According to Figure 4.1, some key programs are given in Figure 4.2.

IV. Flooding

Another static algorithm is flooding, in which every incoming packet is sent out on

```
struct state{
    int predecessor;
    int length;
    int label;
    }state[MAX_NODE];

do{
  for (i=0;i<n;i++)
    if (dist[k][i]!=0 && state[i].label==0){
      if(state[k].length+dist[k][i]<state[i].length) {
                        state[i].predecessor=k;
                        state[i].length=state[k].length+dist[k][i];
                        }
             }
    k=0;min=INFINITY;
    for(i=0;i<n;i++)
    if(state[i].label==0 &&state[i].length<min){
    min=state[i].length;
    k=i;
    }
    state[k].label=1;
} while(k!=s) ;
```

Figure 4. 2   Realization of key codes

every outgoing line except the one it arrived on. [3] Obviously, it generates vast numbers of duplicate packets. Consequently, some measures occur to **damp** this process. One is to have a hop counter contained in the header of each packet. The second technique is putting a sequence number in each packet for avoiding sending them out a second time. Another more practical approach is **selective flooding**, which sends incoming packet out only on those lines that are going approximately in the right direction. [4]

Flooding is not practical in most applications, but it has some applications, such as military applications, distributed database applications.

V. Bellman-Ford algorithm

The distance vector routing algorithm, also called Bellman-Ford algorithm, operates by having each router maintain a table giving the best known distance to each destination and which line to use to get there. [5] These tables are updated by exchanging information with the neighbors every once in a while. It was the original ARPANET routing algorithm and was also used in the Internet under the name RIP. Distance vector routing can work in theory but has a serious drawback in practice: it **converges** to good news fast, but it reacts slowly to bad news. This latter problem is known as the **count-to-infinity** problem.

VI. Link state routing algorithm

The idea of link state routing (LSR) is simple and can be stated as five parts:
- Discover its neighbors and learn their network addresses.
- Measure the delay or cost to each of its neighbors.
- Construct a packet including all it has just learned.
- Send this packet to all other routers.
- Compute the shortest path to every other router.

1. Learning about the Neighbors

Each router learns about its neighbors by sending a special HELLO packet on each point-to-point line.

2. Measuring Line Cost

The most direct way to determine this delay is to send over the line a special ECHO packet that the other side is required to send back immediately. By measuring the round-trip time and dividing it by two, the sending router can get a reasonable estimate of the delay.

3. Building Link State Packets

The link state packet starts with the identity of the sender, followed by a sequence number and age, and a list of neighbors. For each neighbor, the delay to it is given.

4. Distributing the Link State Packets

LSR uses flooding to distribute the link state packets. To keep the flood in check, each packet contains a sequence number that is **incremented** for each new packet sent. ⑥

5. Computing the New Routes

When a router has accumulated a full set of link state packets, the entire subnet graph is constructed and Dijkstra's algorithm is used to construct the shortest path to all possible destinations.

The OSPF protocol, which is widely used in the Internet, is based on the link state routing algorithm.

Notes

① The routing algorithm is responsible for deciding which output line an incoming packet should be transmitted on. 在这个句子中 which 引导定语从句,实际上后面引导的句子正确的顺序应该为 an incoming packet should be transmitted on which output line。

② Given a network of nodes connected by bidirectional links, where each link has a cost associated with it in each direction. 这里的 where 指代前面 in bidirectional links,后半句完整的句子应该是 each link has a cost associated with it in each direction in bidirectional links。

③ Another static algorithm is flooding, in which every incoming packet is sent out on every outgoing line except the one it arrived on. 在这句话中 which 引导定语从句,指代 flooding 算法,后面还有一个定语从句由 that 引导,省略了 that,实际应该是 except the one that it arrived on。

④ Another more practical approach is selective flooding, which sends incoming packet out only on those lines that are going approximately in the right direction. 在这个句子里包含两个定语从句,分别由 which 和 that 引导,which 指代 selective flooding,that 指代 those lines。

⑤ The distance vector routing algorithm, also called Bellman-Ford algorithm, operates by having each router maintain a table giving the best known distance to each destination and which line to use to get there. 在这个句子中 by 后面接了动词的-ing 形式,而此动词 have 的宾语 each router 又引导了一个定语从句,省略了 that,应该是 each router that maintain a table,而 table 又做了后面动词 give 的主语,所以动词 give 以-ing 形式出现整个后面的短语一起修饰 table,give 的宾语有 distance 和后面的 line,而 line 又由一个动词不定式 to use to get there 修饰它。

⑥ To keep the flood in check，each packet contains a sequence number that is incremented for each new packet sent. 在这个句子中 that 引导定语从句指代前面的 sequence number,后面的 sent 是动词的过去分词形式表被动,修饰前面的 packet。

New Words and Phrases

bidirectional	[ˌbaidəˈrekʃənl]	*adj.*	双向的;双向作用的
weight	[weit]	*vt.*	使……负重;使倾斜
adjacent	[əˈdʒeisnt]	*adj.*	邻近的;毗连的;接近的
damp	[dæmp]	*vt.*	使潮湿;使扫兴
converge	[kənˈvɛːdʒ]	vi.	聚合;集中;会聚
increment	[ˈiŋkrəmənt]	*n.*	增量;增加;增值;增额

Computer Terminologies

adaptive algorithm	自适应算法
non-adaptive algorithm	非自适应算法
virtual circuit	虚电路
datagram services	数据报服务
static routing	静态路由
shortest path routing	最短路径路由
flooding	洪泛算法
distance vector routing	距离矢量路由
link state routing	链路状态路由
selective flooding	选择洪泛
count-to-infinity	无穷计算

Exercises

I. Translate the sentences into Chinese.

1. The network layer is concerned with getting packets from the source all the way to the destination.

2. In virtual-circuit subnets，a routing decision is made when the virtual circuit is set up.

3. To achieve these goals，the network layer must know about the topology of the communication subnet and choose appropriate paths through it.

4. Routing algorithms can be grouped into two major classes：non-adaptive and adaptive.

5. Non-adaptive algorithms，also called static routing，do not make decision based on

measurements or estimates of the current traffic and topology.

6. Examples of static routing commonly used are shortest path routing, and flooding.

7. In contrast, adaptive algorithms change their routing decisions to reflect changes in the topology, and usually the traffic as well.

8. Given a network of nodes connected by bidirectional links, where each link has a cost associated with it in each direction.

9. Dijskstra algorithm can be stated as: find the shortest paths from a given source node to all other nodes.

10. Another more practical approach is selective flooding, which sends incoming packet out only on those lines that are going approximately in the right direction.

11. The distance vector routing algorithm, also called Bellman-Ford algorithm, operates by having each router maintain a table giving the best known distance to each destination and which line to use to get there.

12. Distance vector routing can work in theory but has a serious drawback in practice: it converges to good news fast, but it reacts slowly to bad news.

Extending Your Reading

Case history—Cisco system

Cisco currently dominates the Internet router market and in recent years has moved into the Internet telephony market. How did this gorilla of a networking company come to be? It all started in 1984 in the living room of a Silicon Valley apartment.

Len Bosak and his wife Sandy Lerner were working at Stanford University when they had the idea to build and sell Internet routers to research and academic institutions. Sandy Lerner came up with the name Cisco (an abbreviation for San Francisco), and she also designed the company's bridge logo. Corporate headquarters was their living room, and they financed the project with credit cards and moonlighting consulting jobs. At the end of 1986, Cisco's revenues reached $250,000 a month. Over the next few years, Cisco continued to grow and grab more and more market share. At the same time, relations between Bosak/Lerner and Cisco management became strained. In 1990, Bosak and Lerner left the company.

参考译文

路 由 算 法

网络层关心的是从源节点获取分组到目的节点的整个路径。从源节点到目的节点路由分组是网络层的主要工作。网络层向传输层也提供了虚电路服务或者报文服务。在虚电路子网中,当虚电路建立好后,路由决策就制定好了。如果是面向无连接的服务,不提前建立连接。

为了达到这些目的,网络层必须清楚通信子网的拓扑,并选择合适的通过路径。路由算法负责决定发送进来的分组应该传送给哪条输出线路。

路由算法分类

路由算法主要分成两大类:非自适应算法和自适应算法。非自适应算法也叫静态路由,它不根据当前估计和测量的流量和拓扑来做决策。相反,路径的选择已经提早计算好了。经常使用的静态路由的算法有最短路径路由算法、洪泛算法。与之相反,自适应路由算法改变路由决策以反映拓扑的变化,通常也会反映流量的变化。它也被叫做活动路由算法,比如距离矢量路由算法、链路状态算法。

最短路径路由算法

在研究最短路径算法之前,先简单地陈述一个问题,如下:

给定一个网络其节点由双向链路连接,每一条链路的每一个方向都关联着一个费用成本。两个节点之间路径的成本定义为所遍历的链路费用的总和。问题是要为每一对节点找到最低成本路径。

最短路径算法,也叫做 Dijskstra 算法,是一种静态路由算法。Dijskstra 算法规定:为给定的源节点到其他所有的节点找到最短路径。算法分三个阶段进行:初始化、获得下一个节点、更新最少成本路径。为了表明算法是如何工作的,以无向有权图 4.1 为例,这里权重表示距离。目的是找到从 A 到 D 的最短路径。Dijskstra 算法形式描述如下。

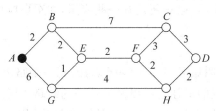

图 4.1   无向加权图

定义:

N——网络中节点集。

S——源节点。

T——算法标记的节点集。

$w(i, j)$——从节点 i 到节点 j 的链路成本。$w(i, j)=0$。如果节点 i 和节点 j 不直接相邻,$w(i, j)=\infty$。

$L(n)$——根据算法,从节点 s 到节点 n 当前最低成本路径费用。

(1) 初始化。$T=\{s\}, L(n)=w(s,n)$。

(2) 获取下一节点。找到 x 满足 $x \notin T$,且 $L(x)=\min_{j \notin T} L(j)$。把 x 加入到集合 T 中。如果 $T=N$,停止。否则,转到步骤(3)。

(3) 更新最低成本路径:对于所有的 $n \notin T, L(n)=\min[L(n), L(x)+w(x,n)]$。转步骤(2)。

根据图 4.1,主要程序代码如图 4.2 所示。

```
struct state{
    int predecessor;
    int length;
    int label;
    }state[MAX_NODE];

do{
 for (i=0;i<n;i++)
  if (dist[k][i]!=0 && state[i].label==0){
   if(state[k].length+dist[k][i]<state[i].length) {
                        state[i].predecessor=k;
                        state[i].length=state[k].length+dist[k][i];
                        }
            }
    k=0;min=INFINITY;
    for(i=0;i<n;i++)
    if(state[i].label==0 &&state[i].length<min){
    min=state[i].length;
    k=i;
    }
    state[k].label=1;
} while(k!=s) ;
```

图 4.2　关键代码实现

洪泛算法

另外一个静态路由算法是洪泛算法,在这个算法中,每一个发送来的分组都被送往所有的除了它发送进来的所有输出线路。明显地,它产生大量的重复的分组。因此,产生一些措施抑制这个过程。一种方法是在每一个分组头部包含一个跳计数器。一种是在每个分组里面放一个序列号避免重复发送第二次。另外还有一种更实际的方法是选择洪泛,把进来的分组只发往可能正确方向的输出线路。

洪泛算法虽然不是很实用,但它还是有一些应用,如军事应用、分布式数据库应用。

Bellman-Ford 路由算法

距离矢量路由算法,也叫做 Bellman-Ford 算法,每一个路由器都维护一个表,它给出了已知的到达每一个目的节点的最佳距离以及所使用的线路。通过不断地与领接节点交换信息来更新这些表。它也是 ARPANET 的最初的路由算法,用在 Internet 的 RIP 的协议中。距离矢量路由算法理论上可以工作,而实际上有一个很严重的缺陷:它对好消息收敛快,对坏消息反应慢。后者导致了无穷计算的问题。

链路状态路由算法

链路状态路由算法的思想简单,说明如下五个部分:
- 找到它的邻居,获取邻居的网络地址。
- 测量到每一个邻居节点的延迟和费用。
- 构造一个分组,包含刚才它所获取的所有信息。
- 把这个分组发送给所有的其他的路由器。
- 计算到每个其他路由器的最短路径。

发现邻居

每一个路由器通过在每一条点对点线路上发送一个特殊的 HELLO 分组,来发现所有的邻居。

测量线路开销

获取延迟的最直接的方法是在线路上发送一个特殊的 ECHO 分组,此分组要求线路的另一端立即应答。通过测量来回的时间除以 2,发送路由器可以获得一个合理的延迟估计。

建立链路状态分组

链路状态分组以发送方的标志开始,接着是一个序列号和年龄,然后是邻居列表。对于每一个邻居,到它的延迟都给出了。

发布链路状态分组

LSR 使用洪泛方法发散链路状态分组。为了监视发散情况,每一个分组包含一个序列号,每发送一个新分组其值加 1。

计算新路由

当一个路由器收集了全套的链路状态分组,整个子网图就可以构造出来,Dijkstra 算法用来构造到所有可能目的节点的最短路径。

OSPF 路由协议广泛用于 Internet 中,是基于链路状态的路由算法。

Section B　The IPv4 Protocol

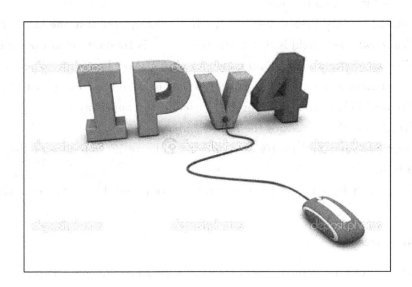

I. The IPv4 Protocol

The IP protocol is the core of the whole Internet，operating in the network layer. An IP datagram consists of a header part and a data part，and its header has a 20-byte fixed part and a variable length optional part. The header format is shown in Figure 4.3.

The *Version* field indicates the version of the protocol. Here it's 0100 in binary.

The *IHL* field is provided to tell how long the header is，in 32-bit words. When no options are present，it has the minimum value 5.

The *Type of service* field is used to distinguish between different classes of service.

The *Total length* field is the length of both header and data，with the maximum

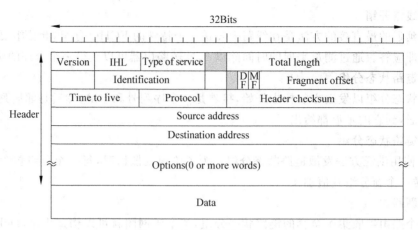

Figure 4.3   The IPv4 header

length 65,535 bytes.

The *Identification* field is needed to allow the destination host to determine which datagram a newly arrived fragment belongs to.

DF stands for Don't Fragment.

MF stands for More Fragments. All fragments except the last one have this bit set.

The *Fragment offset* field is to tell the position this fragment is in the datagram.

The *Time to live* field is a counter used to limit packet lifetimes. When it hits zero, the packet is **discarded** and a warning packet is sent back to the source host.

The *Protocol* field indicates the protocol used in the upper layer.

The *Header checksum* verifies the header only.

The *Source address* and *Destination address* indicate IP addresses of the source and destination host.

The *Options* field was designed to provide some aid functions with the variable length.

II. IPv4 Addresses

Every host and router on the Internet has an IP address, which **encodes** its network number and host number. In principle, no two machines on the Internet have the same IP address. In IPv4 scheme, all IP addresses are 32bits. The allocation of IP addressed uses **classful addressing** and they are divided into five categories, as shown in Figure 4.4. The class A, B and C formats allow for up to 128 networks with 16 million hosts each, 16,384 networks with up to 64K hosts, and 2 million networks with up to 256hosts each, respectively.

The 32-bit IP addresses are usually written in **dotted decimal notation**, and each of 4bytes is written in **decimal**, from 0 to 255. Their network numbers are managed by **ICANN** (Internet Corporation for Assigned Names and Numbers) to avoid conflicts. There are special IP addresses shown in Figure 4.5. The lowest IP address 0.0.0.0 is used by

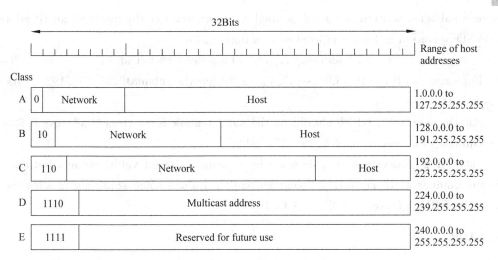

Figure 4.4   IP address formats

hosts when they are being booted, and the highest 255.255.255.255 is broadcast on the local network. All addresses of the form 127.xx.yy.zz are reserved for **loopback** testing.

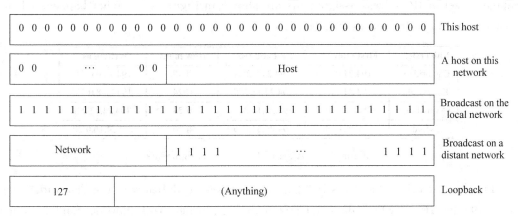

Figure 4.5   Special IP addresses

III. Subnets

From Figure 4.4, we can see that all the hosts in a network must have the same network number, which may cause many problems as networks grow. One of the problems is that a single class A, B, or C address refers to one network, not to a collection of LANs. The solution to deal with it is subnetting, which borrows some bits for subnet-id from the host part in the IP address format.[1] So, the IP address format is split into three parts: network, **subnet** and host number, as shown in Figure 4.6.

Figure 4.6   Subnet format

Subnetting allows a network to be split into several parts for internal use but still act like a single network to the outside world[2]. It has subnet masks for distinguishing between subnets, written in dotted decimal notation. To get the net-id of an IP address, the AND operation in binary is used as equation (4.1).

$$(IP\ address)\ AND\ (subnet\ mask) = net\text{-}id \qquad (4.1)$$

For example, if the IP address 141.14.72.24 has the **submask** 255.255.192.0, its net-id is 141.14.64.0.

Another example: which should be the subnet **mask** for a class C address if 62hosts are required? The answer is 255.255.255.192.

Subnetting reduces router table space by creating a three-level hierarchy, but does not add the number of IP addresses. Next we will introduce some solutions to alleviate the shortage of IP addresses: CIDR, NAT, IPv6.

IV. CIDR

CIDR (Classless InterDomain Routing) is dropping the classes of IP addresses to allocate the remaining IP addresses in **variable-sized** blocks.

Dropping the classes makes forwarding more complicated. Let's take an example. Suppose a set of IP address assignments are shown in Figure 4.7. What happens when a packet comes in addressed to 194.24.17.4?

University	First address	Last address	How many	Written as
Cambridge	194.24.0.0	194.24.7.255	2048	194.24.0.0/21
Edinburgh	194.24.8.0	194.24.11.255	1024	194.24.8.0/22
(Available)	194.24.12.0	194.24.15.255	1024	194.24.12/22
Oxford	194.24.16.0	194.24.31.255	4096	194.24.16.0/20

Figure 4.7　A set of IP address assignments

Firstly, the original address 194.24.17.4 is Boolean **ANDed** with the Cambridge mask to get 194.24.16.0, which does not match the Cambridge base address. Similarly, it is ANDed with the Edinburgh mask, and the result is not matched. So Oxford is tried next, which yields a matched result. If no longer matches are found farther down the table, the Oxford entry is used and the packet is sent along the corresponding line.

V. NAT

NAT (Network Address Translation) is a **long-term** solution for the whole Internet to migrate to IPv6 and is widely used. The basic idea of NAT is to introduce the concept of private IP addresses, assign each company a single IP address for Internet traffic and assign computers within the company the private IP address for routing **intramural** traffic. The three reserved ranges are:

10.0.0.0　　　−10.255.255.255/8　　(16,777,216hosts)

172.16.0.0　　−172.31.255.255/12　(1,048,576hosts)

192.168.0.0　−192.168.255.255/16　(65,536hosts)

No packets containing these private addresses may appear on the Internet itself. When a packet exits the company and goes to the ISP or a packet arrives at the NAT box from the ISP, an address translation takes place. The operation of NAT is shown in Figure 4. 8. TCP ports are also used to make NAT work.

Whenever an outgoing packet enters the NAT box, the 10. x. y. z source address is replaced by the company's true IP address. In addition, the TCP source port field is replaced by the destination port. That is to say, the mapping of the source IP address and port and the destination IP address and port is established. When a packet arrives at the NAT box from the ISP, it can find its destination according to the NAT box's mapping table.

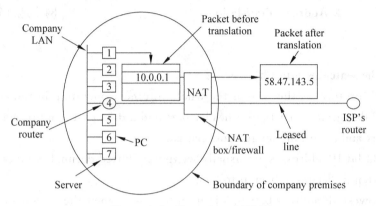

Figure 4. 8　Operation of NAT

Notes

① The solution to deal with it is subnetting, which borrows some bits for subnet-id from the host part in the IP address format. 动词不定式 to deal with it 修饰前面的 solution,which 引导定语从句指代前面的 solution。

② Subnetting allows a network to be split into several parts for internal use but still act like a single network to the outside world. 在这句话中,后半句谓语为 act like,省略了主语,其主语为 several parts。

New Words and Phrases

discard	[dis'kɑːd]	vt.	丢弃;抛弃
encode	[in'kəʊd]	vt.	编码;译码
decimal	['desiməl]	adj.	小数的;十进位的
loopback	[lʊp'bæk]	n.	回送(信号等);回放;回路
subnet	['sʌbnet]	n.	子[分支]网络
subnetting	[sʌb'letiŋ]	n.	划分子网
mask	[mɑːsk]	n.	伪装;面罩;面具;掩码
submask	[səb'mɑːsk]	n.	子掩码

variable-sized		变长的
anded		相与
long-term		长期的;长远
intramural	[ˌintrəˈmjʊərəl]	adj. 校内的;同一组织内的

Computer Terminologies

classful addressing	分类地址
dotted decimal notation	点分十进制表示法
ICANN (Internet Corporation for Assigned Names and Numbers)	互联网名称和编号公司
CIDR (Classless InterDomain Routing)	无类域间路由
NAT (Network Address Translation)	网络地址转换

Exercises

I. Translate the sentences into Chinese.

1. The IP protocol is the core of the whole Internet, operating in the network layer.

2. An IP datagram consists of a header part and a data part, and its header has a 20-byte fixed part and a variable length optional part.

3. The 32-bit IP addresses are usually written in dotted decimal notation, and each of 4bytes is written in decimal, from 0 to 255.

4. The lowest IP address 0.0.0.0 is used by hosts when they are being booted, and the highest 255.255.255.255 is broadcast on the local network.

5. The solution to deal with it is subnetting, which borrows some bits for subnet-id from the host part in the IP address format.

6. It has subnet masks for distinguishing between subnets, written in dotted decimal notation.

7. CIDR (Classless InterDomain Routing) is dropping the classes of IP addresses to allocate the remaining IP addresses in variable-sized blocks.

8. NAT (Network Address Translation) is a long-term solution for the whole Internet to migrate to IPv6 and is widely used.

9. When a packet exits the company and goes to the ISP or a packet arrives at the NAT box from the ISP, an address translation takes place.

10. Whenever an outgoing packet enters the NAT box, the 10.x.y.z source address is replaced by the company's true IP address.

II. Answer the questions.

1. In our text there is an example, "For example, if the IP address 141.14.72.24 has the submask 255.255.192.0, its net-id is 141.14.64.0." Can you give the process of calculating its net-id?

2. In our text there is another example, "Another example: which should be the subnet mask for a class C address if 62hosts are required? The answer is 255.255.255.

192." Can you also give the process of calculating the subnet mask?

3. Describe the basic ideas of NAT.

4. Describe the differences between CIDR and classful addressing.

Extending Your Reading

Principles in practice—Three bears problem

Back in 1987, a few visionaries predicted that some day the Internet might grow to 100,000 networks. Most experts pooh-poohed this as being decades in the future, if ever. The 100,000th network was connected in 1996. The problem is that the Internet is rapidly running out of IP addresses. In principle, over 2 billion addresses exist, but the practice of organizing the address space by classes wastes millions of them. In particular, the real villain is the class B network. For most organizations, a class A network, with 16 million addresses is too big, and a class C network, with 256 addresses is too small. A class B network, with 65,536, is just right. In Internet folklore, this situation is known as the three bears problem.

参考译文

IPv4 协议

IP 协议是整个 Internet 核心,它工作于网络层。一个 IP 数据报包含头部分和数据部分,数据报头有一个固定的 20 个字节长度部分和一个可选的变长部分。数据报头格式如图 4.3 所示。

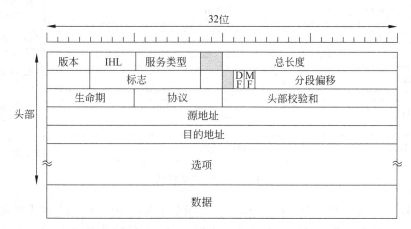

图 4.3　IPv4 头部

- Version(版本)字段表明协议的版本。这里是 0100B。
- IHL 字段用 32 位字表明头部的长度。当没有选项出现时,它有最小值 45。
- Type of service(服务类型)字段用来区分不同类型的服务。
- Total length(总长)字段是包含头和数据的长度,最大值为 65 535 字节。

- Identification(标志)字段用来让目标主机确定新到的片段属于哪个数据报。
- DF 字段代表不允许分段。
- MF 字段代表更多的段。除了最后的段,所有的段都有这一位。
- Fragment offset(段偏离)字段是告诉这个段在数据报的开始位置。
- Time to live(生存期)字段是用来限制分组生命周期的计数器。当它变为 0 时,分组被丢弃,并且一个警告分组被送回源主机。
- Protocol(协议)字段表明上一层使用的协议。
- Header checksum(头校验和)字段只验证报头。
- Source address(源地址)和 Destination address(目标地址)字段表明 IP 报的源主机地址和目标主机地址。
- Options(可选项)字段用可变长度来提供一些辅助功能。

IPv4 地址

Internet 上的每一台主机和路由器都有一个 IP 地址,它包含其网络地址和主机编号。原则上,Internet 上没有任何两台机器具有相同的 IP 地址。在 IPv4 体系中,所有的 IP 地址都是 32 位。IP 地址的分配采用分类地址,它们分成五类,如图 4.4 所示。A、B、C 类分别允许 128 个网络,每一个网络 1600 万台主机;16 384 个网络,每一个网络 64 000 台主机;200 万个网络,每一个网络多达 256 台主机。

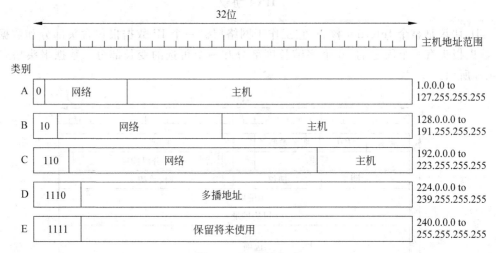

图 4.4　IP 地址格式

32 位 IP 地址经常用点分十进制标记法,每四个字节用一位 0~255 的十进制。为了避免冲突,网络编号由互联网名称和编号公司管理。有一些特殊的 IP 地址如图 4.5 所示。最小的 IP 地址 0.0.0.0 被正在启动的主机使用,最大 IP 地址 255.255.255.255 是局域网的广播地址。所有 127.xx.yy.zz 形式的 IP 地址保留给回路检测使用。

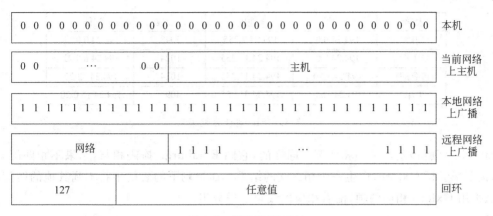

图 4.5   特殊的 IP 地址

子网

从图 4.4 中可以看出位于同一网络中的所有主机必须具有同样的网络号,随着网络的扩展,这可能导致很多的问题。其中一个问题是一个单一的 A 类、B 类或者 C 类是指的一个网络,而不是局域网的集合。解决这个问题的方法是子网,此方法从 IP 地址的主机部分借几位表示子网编号。因此,IP 地址分成三部分:网络地址、子网编号和主机编号,如图 4.6 所示。

网络号	子网号	主机号

图 4.6   子网格式

子网允许一个网络为了使用 Internet 分成多个部分,但是对外看起来仍然像一个网络。它由子网掩码区分不同的子网,采用点分十进制标记法。为了获得一个 IP 地址的网络号,二进制的与运算运用如下。

$$（IP 地址）AND（子网掩码）=网络号 \tag{4.1}$$

比如,如果 IP 地址为 141.14.72.24 具有子网掩码 255.255.192.0,那么它的网络号是 141.14.64.0。

另外一个例子:对于一个 C 类地址,要求有 62 台主机,子网掩码是什么? 答案是 255. 255.255.192。

子网划分通过创建一个三层结构减少了路由表空间,但是不增加 IP 地址数量。接下来介绍缓和 IP 地址缺少的解决方案:CIDR、NAT、IPv6。

CIDR

CIDR(无类域间路由)丢弃 IP 地址的分类用变长块分配剩下的 IP 地址。

丢弃分类使得数据转发更复杂。举个例子。假如 IP 地址集分配如图 4.7 所示。当一个地址为 194.24.17.4 的分组进来,会发生什么呢?

首先,初始地址 194.24.17.4 和 Cambridge 掩码进行布尔与得到 194.24.16.0,它和

大学	首地址	末地址	地址数	记作
剑桥	194.24.0.0	194.24.7.255	2048	194.24.0.0/21
爱丁堡	194.24.8.0	194.24.11.255	1024	194.24.8.0/22
(可分配)	194.24.12.0	194.24.15.255	1024	194.24.12/22
牛津	194.24.16.0	194.24.31.255	4096	194.24.16.0/20

图 4.7 IP 地址分配集

Cambridge(剑桥)基地址不相匹配。同样的,它同 Edinburgh 掩码相与,结果不相匹配。因此,接下来尝试 Oxford,产生一个相匹配的结果。如果剩下的表格中找不到其他的匹配项,那么采用 Oxford 相应的项,沿着相应的线路发送分组。

NAT

NAT(网络地址转换)对于整个网络迁移到 IPv6 地址,是一个长远的解决方案,被广泛使用。NAT 的基本思想是引入私有 IP 地址的概念,为每一个公司分配一个用于因特网数据流的单一的 IP 地址,为公司内部的计算机分配可以在内部路由的私有 IP 地址。三个保留的分段是:

10.0.0.0　　　—10.255.255.255/8　　(16 777 216 主机)

172.16.0.0 　—172.31.255.255/12　 (1 048 576 主机)

192.168.0.0 　—192.168.255.255/16　 (65 536 主机)

没有包含这些私有地址的分组出现在 Internet 上。当一个分组离开公司去往 ISP 或者一个分组从 ISP 到达 NAT 盒,产生一个地址转换。NAT 的操作如图 4.8 所示。也需要 TCP 端口来使得 NAT 工作。

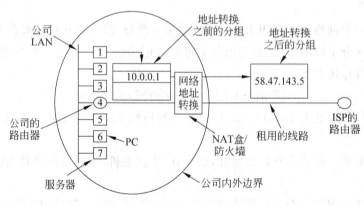

图 4.8 NAT 操作过程

无论何时一个发出去的分组到达一个 NAT 盒,10.x.y.z 源地址转换为公司的真实 IP 地址。另外,TCP 源端口被目的端口取代。也就是说,源 IP 地址和端口到目的 IP 地址和端口映射建立。当一个分组从 ISP 到达 NAT 盒,它可以根据 NAT 盒的映射表找到它的目标地址。

Section C   Internet Control Protocols

I. ICMP

The Internet Control Message Protocol (**ICMP**), is used by hosts, routers, and **gateways** to test the Internet. The most typical use of ICMP is for error reporting. For example, when running a *ping* command, an error **prompt** may occur such as "Destination unreachable", which is reported by the ICMP.① There are a dozen types of ICMP messages defined in RFC 792, some important of which are listed in Figure 4.9. ICMP lies just above IP, and its messages are carried inside IP packets or as IP payload.

Message type	Description
Destination unreachable	Packet could not be delivered
Time exceeded	Time to live field hit 0
Parameter problem	Invalid header field
Source quench	Choke packet
Rediredt	Teach a router about geography
Echo	Ask a machine if it is alive
Echo reply	Yes,I am alive
Timestamp request	Same as Echo request but with timestamp
Timestamp reply	Same as Echo reply,but with timestamp

Figure 4.9   The principal ICMP message types

II. ARP

Although every machine on the Internet has one (or more) IP addresses, these cannot actually be used for sending packets because the data link layer hardware does not understand Internet addresses. So，the MAC address owned by the **NIC**（Network Interface Card）appears. It is also called **Ethernet address**.

The MAC address is 48bits or 6 bytes，normally expressed in **hexadecimal**. The frontier 24-bits are allocated by IEEE，and the later 24-bits are designated by the network equipment manufacturers.

ff：ff：ff：ff：ff：ff	Broadcast address
01：xx：xx：xx：xx：xx	Multicast address
01：00：5 e：xx：xx：xx	IPv4 multicast address

ARP（Address Resolution Protocol）maps the IP address onto the Ethernet address by sending a broadcast packet in the LAN. The advantage of using ARP is that the system does not have to do much except for assigning an IP address to each machine，and ARP does the rest. ARP attacks are to attack networks by making use of the ARP's working principle.

III. RARP

For a given Ethernet address，how to get its IP address? **RARP**（Reverse Address Resolution Protocol）is the first solution. It allows a **newly-booted** workstation to broadcast its Ethernet address. The RARP server looks up the Ethernet address in its configuration files，and sends back the corresponding IP address. However，it has been replaced by **BOOTP** and **DHCP**（Dynamic Host Configuration Protocol），which both support a much greater feature set than RARP.

IV. Routing in the Internet

In addition to protocols mentioned above，the Internet has several protocols used within an AS or between ASes，as shown in Figure 4.10.

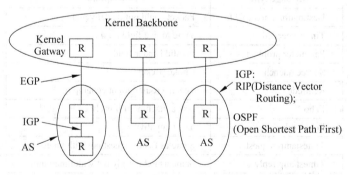

Figure 4.10　Routing in the Internet

1. RIP

The routing information protocol（**RIP**）was one of the earliest **intra-AS** Internet routing protocols and is still in widespread use today. RIP is a distance vector protocol. RIPv2 uses hop count as a cost **metric**，and limits the maximum cost of a path to 15.

That is to say, RIP is used in **autonomous** systems that are less than 15 hops in diameter. In RIP, the routing tables are exchanged between neighbors every 30 seconds.

2. OSPF

The Open Shortest Path First (**OSPF**) routing is also used for intra-AS routing. The "Open" in OSPF indicates the routing protocol specification publicly available. OSPF is a link-state protocol that uses flooding of link state information and a Dijkstra least-cost path algorithm. With OSPF, a router constructs a complete topological map of the entire autonomous system. The router obtains its routing table by using the shortest path algorithm. Compared with RIP, it is adapt to larger autonomous systems with less than 200 hops. [2]

As OSPF autonomous system can be configured into "areas". There are four types of routers: boundary routers, backbone routers, area border routers, internal routers, as shown in Figure 4.11.

- **Boundary routers (BOR):** A boundary router, exchanges routing information with routers belonging to other autonomous systems.
- **Area border routers (ABR):** Connect two or more areas.
- **Backbone routers (BAR):** Within the backbone but themselves are not area border routers.
- **Internal routers (IR):** In a non-backbone areas and only perform intra-AS routing.

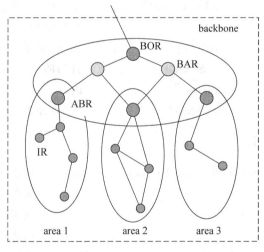

Figure 4.11 Hierarchical Structure of the OSPF AS

3. BGP

BGP (Border Gateway Protocol) is used between autonomous systems. A different protocol is needed between ASes because the goals of an **interior** gateway protocol (**IGP**) and an **exterior** gateway protocol are not the same. An IGP protocol has to do is move packets as efficiently as possible from the source to the destination. But for BGP, there are several elements need to be considered, such as political, security, or economic consideration.

BGP is fundamentally a distance vector protocol, but quite different from RIP. Instead of maintaining just the cost to each destination, each BGP router keeps track of the path used and tells the exact path it is using. [3]

Notes

① The most typical use of ICMP is for error reporting. For example, when running a *ping* command, an error prompt may occur such as "Destination unreachable", which is reported by the ICMP. 在这里 which 引导的定语从句，指代前面的 an error prompt。

② Compared with RIP, it is adapt to larger autonomous systems with less than 200 hops. 这个句子是个省略句，完整的应该是 OSPF is compared with RIP, it is adapt to larger autonomous systems with less than 200 hops.

③ Instead of maintaining just the cost to each destination, each BGP router keeps track of the path used and tells the exact path it is using. 这里介词短语后面接动名词短语做状语，修饰 BGP 路由器的功能不只是记录到每一个目标端的费用；在本句中的 path 后面接 used，修饰前面的 path 表示"被使用的"。

New Words and Phrases

prompt	[prɔmpt]	n.	提示；提示的内容
hexadecimal	[ˌheksə'desiml]	adj.	十六的；十六进制的
newly-booted			新启动地
metric	['metrik]	n.	标准；度量
autonomous	[ɔː'tɔnəməs]	adj.	自治的
interior	[in'tiəriə]	n.	内部
exterior	[ik'stiəriə]	n.	外部；外表

Computer Terminologies

ICMP (Internet Control Message Protocol) Internet	控制信息协议
gateway	网关
NIC (Network Interface Card)	网卡
Ethernet Address	以太网地址
ARP (Address Resolution Protocol)	地址解析协议
RARP (Reverse Address Resolution Protocol)	反向地址解析协议
BOOTP (Bootstrap Protocol)	引导协议
DHCP (Dynamic Host Configuration Protocol)	动态主机配置协议
RIP (Routing Information Protocol)	路由信息协议
intra-As (Autonomous System)	自治系统内部
OSPF (Open Shortest Path First)	开放最短路径优先
BOR (Boundary Routers)	边界路由器

BAR（Backbone Routers）　　　　　　骨干路由器
ABR（Area Border Routers）　　　　区域边界路由器
IR（Internal Routers）　　　　　　内部路由器
BGP（Border Gateway Protocol）　　边界网关协议
IGP（Interior Gateway Protocol）　　内部网关协议

Exercises

Translate the sentences into Chinese.

1. ICMP lies just above IP, and its messages are carried inside IP packets or as IP payload.

2. Although every machine on the Internet has one (or more) IP addresses, these cannot actually be used for sending packets because the data link layer hardware does not understand Internet addresses.

3. The frontier 24-bits are allocated by IEEE, and the later 24-bits are designated by the network equipment manufacturers.

4. ARP (Address Resolution Protocol) maps the IP address onto the Ethernet address by sending a broadcast packet in the LAN.

5. The advantage of using ARP is that the system does not have to do much except for assigning an IP address to each machine, and ARP does the rest.

6. The RARP server looks up the Ethernet address in its configuration files, and sends back the corresponding IP address.

7. That is to say, RIP is used in autonomous systems that are less than 15 hops in diameter.

8. BGP is fundamentally a distance vector protocol, but quite different from RIP.

Extending Your Reading

Principles in practice—Why are three different inter-AS and intra-AS routing protocols?

Why are three different inter-AS and intra-AS routing protocols? The answer to this question gets the heart of the differences between the goals of routing within as AS and among ASs.

- Policy. Among ASs, police issues dominate. It may well be important that traffic originating in a given AS not be able to pass through another specific AS. Similarly, a given AS may well want to control what transit traffic it carries between other ASs. We have know that BGP carries path attributes and provides for controlled distribution of routing information so that such policy-based routing decisions can be made. Within an AS, everything is normally under the same administrative control, and thus policy issues play a much less important role in choosing routes within the AS.

> - Scale. The ability of a routing algorithm and its data structures to scale to handle routing to/among large numbers of networks is a critical issue in inter-AS routing. Within an AS, scalability is less of a concern.
> - Performance. Because inter-AS routing is so policy oriented, the quality of the routes used is often of secondary concern. Indeed, we saw that among ASs, there is not even the notion of cost associated with routes. Within a single AS, however, such policy concerns are of less importance, allowing routing to focus more on the level of performance realized on a route.

参考译文

Internet 控制协议

ICMP

ICMP 被主机、路由器、网关用来测试 Internet。ICMP 最典型的使用是错误报告。比如,当运行一个 ping 命令时,会出现错误提示如"Destination unreachable",这就是由 ICMP 报告。在 RFC 792 中定义了很多的 ICMP 信息,一些重要的列在图 4.9 中。ICMP 位于 IP 上层,它的信息包含在 IP 分组里或者作为 IP 的负载。

信息类型	说明
目标不可达	不能递交分组
超时	TTL值为0
参数问题	无效的头域
源端抑制	抑制分组
重定向	告诉路由器有关地理信息
请求	问一台机器是否还活着
应答	还存活
时间戳请求	同请求,加时间戳
时间戳应答	同应答,加时间戳

图 4.9 ICMP 消息类型

ARP

虽然 Internet 上的每一台机器都有一个或多个 IP 地址,但是这些地址不能用来传输分组,因为数据链路层的硬件无法识别 Internet 地址。因此,网卡上的 MAC 地址出现了。也叫做以太网地址。

MAC 地址是 48 位或 6 字节,一般用十六进制表达。前面 24 位由 IEEE 分配,后面 24 位由网络设备厂商指定。

ff：ff：ff：ff：ff：ff　　　　　广播地址

01：xx：xx：xx：xx：xx　　　　组播地址

01:00:5 e: xx: xx: xx   IPv4 组播地址

ARP(地址解析协议)通过在 LAN 中发送广播,把 IP 地址映射为以太网地址。ARP 的优势是系统除了给机器分配一个 IP 地址外,没有必要考虑更多,剩下的由 ARP 来处理。ARP 攻击是通过利用 ARP 的工作原理来攻击网络。

RARP

给定一个以太网地址,如何获得它的 IP 地址呢? RARP(反向地址解析协议)是首选解决方案。它允许新启动的工作站广播它的以太网地址。RARP 服务器在配置文件中查找它的以太网地址,传回其对应的 IP 地址。虽然如此,RARP 已经被 BOOTP(引导协议)和DHCP(动态主机配置协议)所取代了,这两个协议比 RARP 支持更大的功能集。

Internet 中的路由

除了上面提到的协议,还有许多使用在自治系统内部或自治系统之间的协议,如图 4.10 所示。

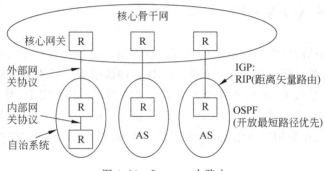

图 4.10 Internet 中路由

RIP

RIP(路由信息协议)是最早的自治系统内 Internet 路由协议,现在仍然广泛使用。RIP是一种距离矢量路由协议。RIPv2 使用跳数作为开销度量,限制路径开销的最大值为 15。

也就是说,RIP 用在最长跳数不超过 15 的自治系统中。在 RIP 中,相邻的站点之间每隔 30 秒交换一次路由表。

OSPF

OSPF(开放最短路径优先路由算法)也用于自治系统内部。OSPF 中的"开放"表明路由协议规范是公开的。OSPF 是一种链路状态协议,它使用了链路状态信息的扩散和Dijkstra 最低成本路径算法。使用 OSPF 协议,路由器构造整个自治系统完整的拓扑图。路由器通过最短路径算得到它的路由表。与 RIP 相比,OSPF 使合于少于 200 跳的更大的自治系统。

因为 OSPF 自治系统可以被配置成区域,相对应,有四种路由器:边界路由器、主干路由器、区域边界路由器、内部路由器,如图 4.11 所示。

- 边界路由器:边界路由器与其他自治系统中的路由器交换路由信息。
- 区域边界路由器:连接两个或者多个区域。

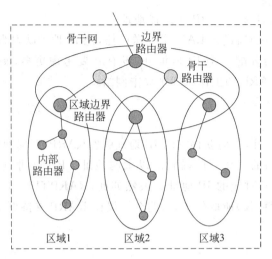

图 4.11　OSPF 自治系统分级结构

- 主干路由器：在主干区域中，但是本身不是区域边界路由器。
- 内部路由器：位于非主干区域，只实施自治系统内部路由。

BGP

BGP（边界网关协议）用于自治系统之间。自治系统之间需要一个不同的协议，因为内部网关协议的目标和外部网关的不是一致的。IGP 协议必须尽可能高效地从源节点移动分组到目的节点。但是对于 BGP，有几个因素需要考虑到，如政治、安全、经济。

BGP 根本上是一个距离矢量协议，但是完全不同于 RIP。每一个 BGP 路由器记录了使用的路径，告诉了正在使用的详细路径，而不是只维持到每一个目标端的费用。

Section D　IPv6 Packet Format

I. Introduction

The format of the IPv6 packet is shown in Figure 4.12. Some important changes have taken place in the IPv6 packet format:

- Larger address space. IPv6 increases the size of the IP address from 32 to 128bits, which insures that the world won't run out of IP addresses. [1]
- Flexible header format.
- Improved options.
- Extended address hierarchy.

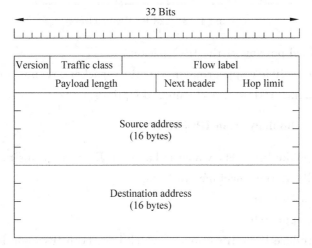

Figure 4.12　IPv6 packet format

A number of IPv4 fields have been dropped or made **optional**. The resulting 40-byte fixed-length header allows for faster processing of the IP packet and a new **encoding** of options allows for more flexible options processing.

The fields of a packet in IPv6 are defined as follows.

Version: always 6 for IPv6.

Traffic class: is used to distinguish between packets with different **real-time** delivery requirements.

Flow label: is still experimental.

Payload length: to tell how many bytes follow the 40-byte header of IPv6.

Next header: to identify the protocol to which the contents (data field) of this packet will be delivered.

Hop limit: is used to keep packets from living forever. It is **decremented** by one by each router that forwards the packet. If the value of **hop** limit reaches zero, the packet is discarded.

Source address and **Destination address**: 16-byte addresses, written as eight groups of four **hexadecimal** digits with colons between the groups. For example, 8000:0000:0000: 0000:0123:4567:89AB:CDEF. The structure of IPv6 addresses is shown in Figure 4.13.

Since many addresses will have many zeros inside them, three **optimizations** have been authorized. First, leading zeros within a group can be omitted, so 0123 can be written as

123. Second，one or more groups of 16 zero bits can be replaced by a pair of **colons**. For example，the above address may become 8000：：123：4567：89AB：CDEF. Finally，IPv4 addresses can be written as a pair of colons and an old dotted decimal number. For example，：：192. 31. 20. 46.

Figure 4. 13 128-bit IPv6 address

Data：the payload portion of the IPv6 packet.

There are several fields appearing in the IPv4 packet are no longer present in the IPv6，those are Fragmentation，Checksum and Options.

II. The transition technology from IPv4 to IPv6

How will the public Internet，which is based on IPv4，be transitioned to IPv6?

(1) **Upgrade** all Internet machines to IPv6.

It needs at least 20 years.

(2) Dual stack approach.

It needs to introduce IPv6/IPv4 nodes，which have both IPv6 and IPv4 addresses，and have the ability to send and receive both IPv4 and IPv6 packets. Figure 4. 14 illustrates the process of the **dual stack approach**.

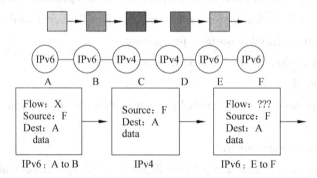

Figure 4. 14 A dual stack approach

(3) Tunneling technology.

The basic idea behind tunneling is the following. Suppose two IPv6 nodes want to **interoperate** using IPv6 packets，but are connected to each other by intervening IPv4 routers. We refer to the intervening set of IPv4 routers between two IPv6 routers as a **tunnel**，as shown in Figure 4. 15. With tunneling，the IPv6 node on the sending side of the tunnel (e. g. ，B) takes the entire IPv6 packet，and puts it in the data field of an IPv4 packet. This IPv4 packet is then addressed to the IPv6 node on the receiving side of the tunnel (e. g. ，E) and sent to the first node in the tunnel (e. g. ，C). The **intervening** IPv4 routers in the tunnel route this IPv4 packet，without realizing the IPv4 packet containing a complete IPv6 packet. ② The IPv6 node on the receiving side of the tunnel eventually receives the IPv4 packet，determines that the IPv4 packet contains an IPv6 packet，extracts the IPv6 packet and then routes the IPv6 packet to its destination.

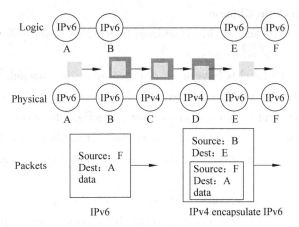

Figure 4.15　Tunneling

Notes

① IPv6 increases the size of the IP address from 32 to 128bits，which insures that the world won't run out of IP addresses. 这里 run out of 表示"用尽"的意思，这里 which 引导定语从句指代 128 位，表示 128 位的 IP 地址可以保证世界上的 IP 地址完全够用。

② The intervening IPv4 routers in the tunnel route this IPv4 packet，without realizing the IPv4 packet containing a complete IPv6 packet. 介词 without 后面接了动词的 ing 形式，而其后的宾语 IPv4 packet 被动名词 containing a complete IPv6 packet 修饰。

New Words and Phrases

optional	['ɔpʃənl]	adj.	任选的
encode	[in'kəud]	vt.	编码；译码
real-time	['ri:l'taim]	adj.	实时的
decrement	['dekrimənt]	n.	渐减；减少；减少量
hop	[hɔp]	n.	跳跃；单脚跳
hexadecimal	[ˌheksə'desiml]	adj.	十六的；十六进制的
optimization	[ˌɔptimai'zeiʃən]	n.	优化；最佳化
colon	['kəulən]	n.	冒号；结肠
upgrade	[ˌʌp'greid]	vt.	升级；提高；改善
interoperate	[ˌintə'ɔpəreit]	n.	互操作
intervening	[ˌintə'vi:niŋ]	adj.	介于中间的；发生于其间的

Computer Terminologies

dual stack approach	双协议栈方法

| tunnel technology | 隧道技术 |

Exercises

Translate the sentences into Chinese.

1. IPv6 increases the size of the IP address from 32 to 128bits，which insures that the world won't run out of IP addresses.

2. A number of IPv4 fields have been dropped or made optional.

3. The resulting 40-byte fixed-length header allows for faster processing of the IP packet and a new encoding of options allows for more flexible options processing.

4. It is decremented by one by each router that forwards the packet.

5. Since many addresses will have many zeros inside them，three optimizations have been authorized.

6. Second，one or more groups of 16 zero bits can be replaced by a pair of colons.

7. There are several fields appearing in the IPv4 packet are no longer present in the IPv6，those are Fragmentation，Checksum and Options.

8. Suppose two IPv6 nodes want to interoperate using IPv6 packets，but are connected to each other by intervening IPv4 routers.

Extending Your Reading

Case history—Origin of IPv6

With rapid development of the Internet，the shortcomings of IPv4 addressing and irrationality of address allocation lead current IPv4 address to exhaustion in February of this year. Fortunately，in 1990，IETF（International Engineering Task Force） began to plan the next generation internet protocol and set up the IPng（IP-the next generation）working group. In 1996，with establishment of the standards such as RFC 2460，IPv6 protocol was formally published.

参考译文

IPv6 分组格式

引言

IPv6 的格式如图 4.12 所示。IPv6 的分组格式中有一些重要的改变：

- 更大的地址空间。IPv6 把 IP 地址的长度从 32 位增加到了 128 位，保证了 IP 地址不会枯竭。
- 灵活的头部格式。
- 改进了可选项。
- 扩展了地址的层次。

一些 IPv4 的字段被丢弃了或者成了可选项，使得 IPv6 头部变成了 40 字节固定长度。

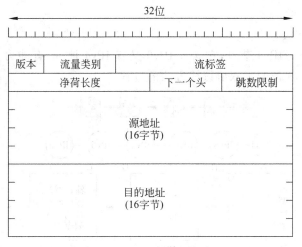

图 4.12　IPv6 分组格式

这样长度的头部允许 IP 分组处理更快,可选项新的编码方式允许更灵活的选项处理。

IPv6 的分组字段如下。

- Version(版本):一般 IPv6 中这个值是 6。
- Traffic class(流量类别):用来区分不同实时要求转发的分组。
- Flow label(流标记):仍然在测试阶段。
- Payload length(负载长度):说明有多少字节跟在 40 字节的 IPv6 头后面。
- Next header(下一个头部):用来表明该分组的内容用来发送给哪个协议。
- Hop limit(跳数限制):用来表明分组的生存期限。它由转发它的每一个路由器减 1。如果此字段的值变为 0,那么丢弃此分组。
- Source address and Destination address(源地址和目标地址):16 字节的地址,写成 8 组每组 4 个十六进制数的形式,每一组用冒号隔开。比如,8000:0000:0000: 0000:0123:4567:89AB:CDEF。IPv6 地址的结构如图 4.13 所示。

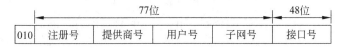

图 4.13　128 位 IPv6 地址

由于很多地址包含了很多 0 在里面,提出三种优化方法可以使用。第一种,以 0 开头的分组中的 0 可以被省略,因此 0123 可以写出 123。第二种,一组或者多组 16 位 0 比特的分组可以被一对冒号代替。例如,上面的地址可以变成 8000::123:4567:89AB:CDEF。第三种,IPv4 地址可以写成一对冒号加上老的点分十进制数,如::192.31.20.46。

- Data(数据):IPv6 分组的负载部分。

有几个出现在 IPv4 里面的字段不再出现在 IPv6 里面,它们是分段、校验和、可选项。

IPv4 到 IPv6 的过渡技术

公用的基于 IPv4 的 Internet 怎样过渡到 IPv6 呢?

(1) 所有的 Internet 机器升级到 IPv6。

它至少需要 20 年。

（2）双协议栈方法。

它需要引入 IPv6/IPv4 节点，它既有 IPv6 又有 IPv4 地址，有能力发送和接收 IPv4 和 IPv6 的分组。图 4.14 说明了双协议栈方法的过程。

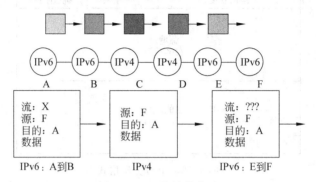

图 4.14　双协议栈方法

（3）隧道技术。

隧道技术背后的思想如下。假如 2 个 IPv6 节点要交互操作 IPv6 分组，但是中间通过 IPv4 路由器相互连接。我们把在两个 IPv6 路由器之间的 IPv4 路由器集合构成一个隧道，如图 4.15 所示。采用隧道技术，隧道发送端的 IPv6 节点（如 B），把整个的 IPv6 分组放在 IPv4 分组的数据字段里。这个 IPv4 分组寻址隧道接收端的 IPv6 节点（如 E），发送给隧道的第一个节点（如 C）。隧道中间的 IPv4 路由器路由此 IPv4 分组，不需要知道 IPv4 分组中包含一个完整的 IPv6 分组。隧道接收端的 IPv6 节点最终收到 IPv4 分组，确定 IPv4 分组里 IPv6 分组，抽取其中的 IPv6，然后把 IPv6 路由到它的目的地。

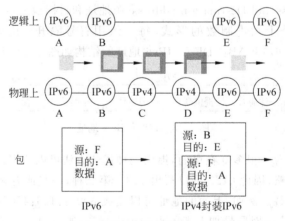

图 4.15　隧道

Unit 5   The Transport Layer

Section A   The Transport Service and UDP

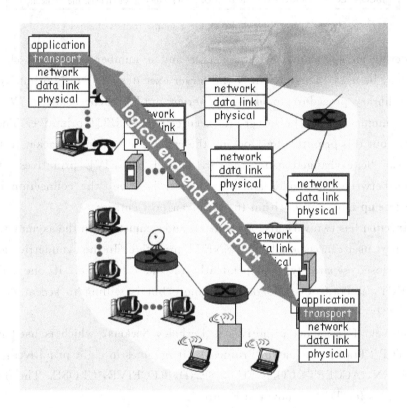

I. The transport service

The transport layer is the heart of the whole protocol hierarchy, whose task is to provide reliable, **cost-effective** data transport from the source machine to the destination machine. It provides services to the application layer, which is implemented by the transport **entity** using transport service **primitives.** [1]

1. Transport entity

Transport entity is the hardware and/or software within the transport layer that does the work. It can be located in the operating system **kernel** or in a **library package** to the application layer.

2. Transport Service Primitives

To allow users to access the transport service, it must provide some operations to application programs. Each transport service, also called primitive, is done by its own interface. The simplest transport service primitive is shown in Figure 5.1.

Primitive	Packet sent	Meaning
LISTEN	(none)	Block until some process tries to connect
CONNECT	CONNECTION REQ.	Actively attempt to establish a connection
SEND	DATA	Send information
RECEIVE	(none)	Block until a DATA packet arrives
DISCONNECT	DISCONNECTION REQ.	This side wants to release the connection

Figure 5.1   The primitives for a simple transport service

Considering an application with a server and a number of remote clients, these primitives may be used. To start with, the server executes a LISTEN primitive, typically by calling a library procedure to **block** the server until a client comes.[②] When a client wants to communicate with the server, it executes a CONNECT primitive. The transport entity carries out this primitive by blocking the caller and sending a packet to the server. Now data can be exchanged using the SEND and RECEIVE primitives. When data transmission between the sender and the receiver is done, the connection is must be released to **free up** table space within the two transport entities.

Disconnection has two **variants**: **asymmetric** and **symmetric**. In the asymmetric variant, either transport user can issue a DISCONNECT primitive. In the symmetric variant, each direction is closed separately, independently of the other one. If one side sends a DISCONNECT, it does not send data any more but is willing to accept data from its partner.

Another set of transport primitives is Berkeley **Sockets**, which is used in Berkeley UNIX for TCP (Transport Control Protocol). It involves in eight primitives: SOCKET, BIND, LISTEN, ACCEPT, CONNECT, SEND, RECEIVE, CLOSE. The flow chart of Berkeley Sockets for TCP is shown in Figure 5.2.

II. UDP

There are two protocols available in the transport layer to its applications: UDP and TCP. Now let's study how UDP works.

1. The UDP protocol

UDP (User Datagram Protocol) is **connectionless** and provides a way for applications to send data without having to establish a connection. UDP transmits segments consisting of an 8-byte header followed by the payload. Its header is shown in Figure 5.3.

The *source port* and the *destination port* field are used to **specify** which process on the sending/receiving machine for sending back a reply.

The *length field* includes the 8-byte header and the data.

The *checksum* is optional and stored as 0 if not computed.

Compared with TCP, UDP is a connectionless service and lacks congestion control.

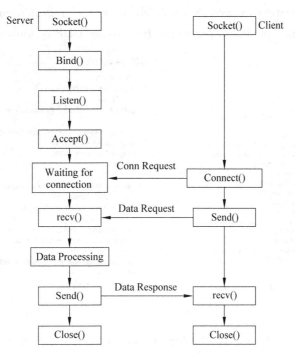

Figure 5.2　Flow Chart of Socket for TCP

Figure 5.3　The UDP header

But UDP has its own features, such as small segment header **overhead** and **unregulated** send rate. It is also commonly used today with multimedia applications, such as Internet phone, real-time video conferencing, and streaming of stored audio and video.

2. An example of UDP applications

DNS is an example of an application-layer protocol that uses UDP.

When the DNS application in a host wants to make a query, it constructs a DNS query message and passes the message to a UDP socket. Without performing any handshaking, UDP adds a header fields to the message and passes the resulting segment to the network layer. The network layer **encapsulates** the UDP **segment** into a **datagram** and sends the datagram to a name server. The DNS application at the querying host then waits for a reply to its query. If it doesn't receive a reply, it either tries sending the query to another name-server, or it informs the invoking application that it can't get a reply.

In practice, DNS almost always runs over UDP.

3. UDP client-server programming

Here we present the application of UDP in Java. The reason has two: first, it is more neatly and cleanly written in Java. Second，client-server programming in Java is becoming increasingly popular. The client/server program using UDP is shown in Figure 5.4.

UDPClient.java

```
import java.io.*;
import java.net.*;
class UDPClient {
public static void main(String args[]) throws Exception
{
BufferedReader inFromUser =
new BufferedReader(new InputStreamReader(System.in));
DatagramSocket clientSocket = new DatagramSocket();
InetAddress IPAddress = InetAddress.getByName("hostname");
byte[] sendData = new byte[1024];
byte[] receiveData = new byte[1024];
String sentence = inFromUser.readLine();
sendData = sentence.getBytes();
DatagramPacket sendPacket =
new DatagramPacket(sendData, sendData.length, IPAddress,9876);
clientSocket.send(sendPacket);
DatagramPacket receivePacket =
new DatagramPacket(receiveData, receiveData.length);
clientSocket.receive(receivePacket);
String modifiedSentence =
new String(receivePacket.getData());
System.out.println("FROM SERVER:" + modifiedSentence);
clientSocket.close();
  }
}
```

UDPServer.java

```
import java.io.*;
import java.net.*;
class UDPServer {
public static void main(String args[]) throws Exception
{
DatagramSocket serverSocket = new DatagramSocket(9876);
byte[] receiveData = new byte[1024];
byte[] sendData = new byte[1024];
while(true)
{
DatagramPacket receivePacket =new DatagramPacket(receiveData, receiveData.length);
serverSocket.receive(receivePacket);
String sentence = new String(receivePacket.getData());
InetAddress IPAddress = receivePacket.getAddress();
int port = receivePacket.getPort();
String capitalizedSentence = sentence.toUpperCase();
sendData = capitalizedSentence.getBytes();
DatagramPacket sendPacket =new DatagramPacket(sendData, sendData.length, IPAddress,
port);
serverSocket.send(sendPacket);
    }
  }
}
```

Figure 5.4 Implementation of UDP programming

Notes

① It provides services to the application layer，which is implemented by the transport entity using transport service primitives. 这句话中的 which 指代前面的 services，由传输实体实现；using 动词的 ing 形式，整个动词短语修饰前面的 entity。

② To start with，the server executes a LISTEN primitive，typically by calling a library procedure to block the server until a client comes. 在这个句子中，主语是 server，谓语是 execute，宾语是 primitive，其他的都是修饰成分，介词 by 接动名词短语修饰主语 server，在动名词短语里还包含一个 until 引导的从句修饰其前面的阻塞的服务器。

New Words and Phrases

cost-effective	[ˌkɔstiˈfektiv]	adj.	有成本效益的；划算的
entity	[ˈentəti]	n.	实体；存在；本质
primitive	[ˈprimətiv]	n.	文艺复兴前的艺术家；原始人
kernel	[ˈkɜːnl]	n.	核心；仁；中心；精髓
block	[blɔk]	v.	阻塞
free up			释放
disconnection	[ˌdiskəˈnekʃən]	n.	断开
variant	[ˈveəriənt]	n.	变体
asymmetric	[ˌeisiˈmetrik]	adj.	不对称的
symmetric	[siˈmetrik]	adj.	对称的；匀称的
connectionless	[kəˈnekʃnles]	n.	无连接

specify	['spesifai]	v.	详细说明;指定;阐述
overhead	['əʊuvəhed]	n.	经常开支;普通用费;总开销
unregulate	[ˌʌn'regjuleitid]	adj.	不规范的;紊乱的;不受管理的
encapsulate	[in'kæpsjuleit]	v.	装入胶囊;封进内部;压缩;概括
segment	['segmənt]	n.	部分;弓形;瓣;段;节
datagram	['detəˌgræm]	n.	数据包;数据报

Computer Terminologies

library package	程序包
Sockets	套接字
UDP (User Datagram Protocol)	用户数据报协议

Exercises

Answer the questions.

1. Describe the differences between UDP and TCP.

2. What does the service primitives mean?

3. What does the transport service supply and list them and explain?

4. Tell the differences between asymmetric variant disconnection and symmetric variant disconnection.

5. Which kind of programming language is commonly used in UDP client-server programming.

6. Give some examples of UDP applications.

Extending Your Reading

Case history—Vinton Cerf, Robert Kahn and TCP/IP

In the early 1970's, packet-switched networks began to proliferate, with the ARPAnet—the precursor of the Internet—being just one of many networks. Each of these networks had its own protocol. Two researchers, Vinton Cerf and Robert Kahn recognized the importance of interconnecting these networks and invented a cross-network protocol called TCP/IP, which stands for Transmission Control Protocol/Internet Protocol. The TCP/IP protocol, which is the bread and butter of today's Internet, was devised before PCs and workstations, the web, streaming audio, and chat. Cerf and Kahn saw the need for a networking protocol that, on the one hand, provides broad support for yet-to-be-defined applications and, on the other hand, allows arbitrary hosts and link-layer protocols to interoperate.

参考译文

传输服务和用户数据报协议

传输服务

传输层是整个分层协议的核心,它的任务是为源主机到目标主机提供可信的、成本有效的数据传输。它为应用层提供服务,由传输层通过传输服务原语来实现。

传输实体

传输实体是实现任务的位于传输层的硬件或者软件。它可能位于操作系统内核或者位于应用层的库程序包中。

传输服务原语

为了让用户接入传输服务,它必须向应用程序提供一些操作。也就是,每一个传输服务由它的接口来实现,叫做原语。最简单的传输服务原语如图 5.1 所示。

原语	发送的分组	含义
LISTEN	(无)	阻塞,直到有进程与它建立连接
CONNECT	CONNECTION REQ.	主动尝试建立一个连接
SEND	DATA	发送信息
RECEIVE	(没有)	阻塞,直到一个分组信息到来
DISCONNECT	DISCONNECTION REQ.	释放一个已建立的连接

图 5.1 简单传输服务原语

考虑带一台服务器多台远程客户端的应用,就要用到这些原语。开始,服务器执行 LISTEN 原语,典型地通过呼叫库程序阻塞服务器直到某个客户端到来。当某个客户端想要与服务器通信,它执行 CONNECT 原语。传输层实体通过阻塞调用者以及发送分组给服务器执行此原语。现在,数据可以通过使用 SEND 和 RECEIVE 原语进行交换了。当数据传输在发送者和接收者之间完成,两个传输实体之间的连接必须被释放以释放表空间。

断掉连接有两种方式:非对称和对称。在非对称方式中,任何的传输用户都可以发起一个 DISCONNECT 原语。在对称方式中,每一方都是单独关闭,独立于另外一方。如果一方发送了一个 DISCONNECT,它不再发送任何数据,但是它仍能从另一方接收数据。

另一套传输原语是 Berkely 套接字,它用于 Berkely UNIX 的传输控制协议。它涉及 8 个原语:SOCKET、BIND、LISTEN、ACCEPT、CONNECT、SEND、RECEIVE 和 CLOSE。用于传输控制协议的 Berkeley 套接字流程图如 5.2 所示。

UDP

传输层有两种可用的协议提供应用:UDP 和 TCP。现在学习 UDP 是如何工作的。

UDP 协议

UDP 是无连接的,为应用提供了一种发送数据不需要建立连接的方式。UDP 传输分段,它包含 8 字节的头部,接着是负载。它的头部如图 5.3 所示。

源端口和目标端口字段用来确定发送或者接收机器上哪个进程用来发送答复。

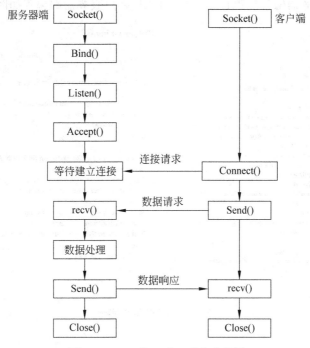

图 5.2　TCP 的 Socket 通信流程图

图 5.3　UDP 头部格式

长度字段包括了 8 字节的头部以及数据。

校验和字段是可选项,如果无计算,其值是 0。

与 TCP 相比,UDP 是一个无连接服务,缺少拥塞控制。但是 UDP 有自己的特点,如小的段报头开销,没有规定的发送速率。如今,它经常用于多媒体应用,如网络电话、实时视频会议、以及流媒体存储音频和视频。

一个 UDP 应用例子

DNS 是一个应用层协议使用 UDP 的例子。

当主机中的 DNS 应用想要发起一个查询,它构造一个 DNS 查询消息,并把消息发送给 UDP 套接字。不需要任何握手,UDP 对消息增加一个头字段,把结果段发送给网络层。网络层把 UDP 段封装为数据报,并把数据报发给命名服务器。查询端主机上的 DNS 等待查询的回复。如果它没有收到回复,将会尝试向另外的命名服务器发送查询,或者它通知发起程序,它不能得到回复。

实际上,DNS 一直运行在 UDP 之上。

UDP 客户-服务器编程

这里用 Java 语言来描述 UDP 的应用。理由有两点:其一,采用 Java 语言更简洁干净。

其二,Java 客户-服务器编程变得日益流行。UDP 客户服务器端编程如图 5.4 所示。

```
UDPClient.java

import java.io.*;
import java.net.*;
class UDPClient {
public static void main(String args[]) throws Exception
{
BufferedReader inFromUser =
new BufferedReader(new InputStreamReader(System.in));
DatagramSocket clientSocket = new DatagramSocket();
InetAddress IPAddress = InetAddress.getByName("hostname");
byte[] sendData = new byte[1024];
byte[] receiveData = new byte[1024];
String sentence = inFromUser.readLine();
sendData = sentence.getBytes();
DatagramPacket sendPacket =
new DatagramPacket(sendData, sendData.length, IPAddress, 9876);
clientSocket.send(sendPacket);
DatagramPacket receivePacket =
new DatagramPacket(receiveData, receiveData.length);
clientSocket.receive(receivePacket);
String modifiedSentence =
new String(receivePacket.getData());
System.out.println("FROM SERVER:" + modifiedSentence);
clientSocket.close();
    }
}
```

```
UDPServer.java

import java.io.*;
import java.net.*;
class UDPServer {
public static void main(String args[]) throws Exception
{
DatagramSocket serverSocket = new DatagramSocket(9876);
byte[] receiveData = new byte[1024];
byte[] sendData = new byte[1024];
while(true)
{
DatagramPacket receivePacket = new DatagramPacket(receiveData, receiveData.length);
serverSocket.receive(receivePacket);
String sentence = new String(receivePacket.getData());
InetAddress IPAddress = receivePacket.getAddress();
int port = receivePacket.getPort();
String capitalizedSentence = sentence.toUpperCase();
sendData = capitalizedSentence.getBytes();
DatagramPacket sendPacket = new DatagramPacket(sendData, sendData.length, IPAddress, port);
serverSocket.send(sendPacket);
    }
  }
}
```

图 5.4　UDP 编程实现

Section B　TCP and its Congestion Control

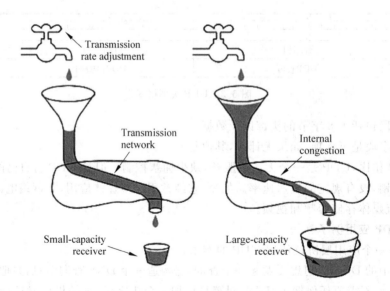

I. TCP

TCP (Transmission Control Protocol) operates in the transport layer, and is designed to provide a **reliable** end-to-end byte **stream** transmission over an unreliable internetwork. The internetworks may differ from each other in topologies, bandwidths, delays, packet sizes, and other parameters. TCP can dynamically adapt to these properties and is **robust** in the face of many kinds of failures. It is formally defined in RFC 793.

1. Sockets and ports

TCP provides services to the application layer. TCP service is obtained by both the sender and receiver creating end points, called sockets.[①] A socket consists of the IP address of the host and its 16-bit port number. A TCP connection is identified **uniquely** by two ends in communication. That is, TCP connection = {socket1, socket2} = {(IP1: port1), (IP2: port2)}.

A port is the TCP name for a **TSAP** (Transport Service Access Point) and is just used to identify the process of the application layer. Generally, ports can be divided into three categories:

- Well-known ports: 0~1023, reserved for standard services. A few of the better known services are listed in Figure 5.5.
- Registered ports: 1024~49151, reserved for application programs without well-known ports.
- Client ports: 49152~65535, reserved for client processes and used temporarily.

2. The TCP protocol

One of key features of TCP is that every byte on a TCP connection has its own 32-bit

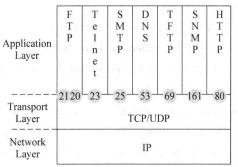

Figure 5.5   Some assigned ports

sequence number, which is used for **acknowledgements** and for the window mechanism. TCP exchanges data in the form of segments. Every segment begins with a **fixed-format**, 20-byte header, shown in Figure 5.6.

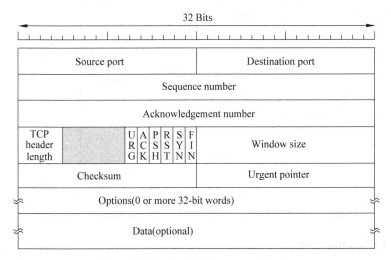

Figure 5.6   The TCP Segment Header

The *Source port* and *Destination port* fields identify the local end points of the connection.

The *Sequence number* field is the number of the sending data.

The *Acknowledgement number* field specifies the number of the next byte expected, not the last byte correctly received.

The *TCP header length* tells how many 32-bit words are contained in the TCP header.

Next there are a 6-bit field that is not used, and *six 1-bit* flags. URG is set to 1 if the Urgent pointer is in use. The *ACK* bit is set to 1 to indicate that the Acknowledgement number is valid. The *PSH* bit indicates PUSHed data. The *RST* bit is used to reset a connection that has become confused. The *FIN* bit is used to **release** a connection. It specifies that the sender has no more data to transmit.

The *Window size* field tells how many bytes may be sent starting at the byte acknowledged. [2]

A *Checksum* is also provided for extra reliability.

3. TCP Connection Establishment

Connections are **established** in TCP by means of the **three-way handshake** between the server and the client. Firstly, the server passively waits for an incoming connection by executing the primitives of LISTEN and ACCEPT. Then, the client executes a CONNECT primitive. The CONNECT primitive sends a TCP segment with the SYN bit on and ACK bit off and waits for a response. [3] When the server receives this segment, it can either accept or reject the connection. If it accepts, an acknowledgement segment is sent back. The establishment process of the TCP connection in the normal case is shown in Figure 5.7.

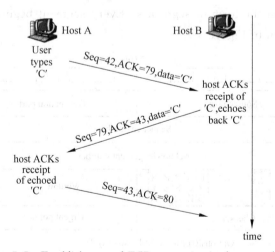

Figure 5.7　Establishment of TCP connection in the normal case

4. TCP Connection Release

To release a connection, either client or server can send a TCP segment with the FIN bit set, which means no more data to transmit. When the FIN is acknowledged, the data transmission in that direction is shut down. However, data may continue to flow indefinitely in the other direction. When the transmissions in both directions have been shut down, the connection is released. Normally, four TCP segments are needed to release a connection, as shown in Figure 5. 8. If the first ACK and the second FIN can be contained in the same segment, the number of TCP segments is reduced to three.

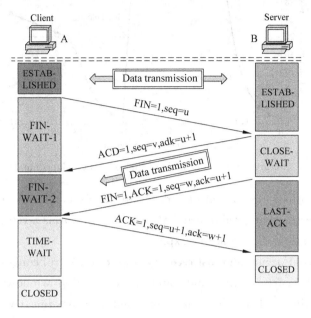

Figure 5. 8　TCP connection release

II. TCP Congestion Control

Because of the limitation of network capacity and receiver capacity, **congestion** appears when the load offered to any network is more than it can handle.[①] To solve these problems, some methods have been proposed: slow start, congestion avoidance, fast retransmit and fast recovery. Among them, the sender maintains two windows and a parameter: the window the receiver has granted, the congestion window, and the **threshold**.

When a connection is established, the sender initializes the congestion window to the size of the maximum segment in use on the connection. It then sends one maximum segment. The congestion window keeps growing **exponentially** until either a **timeout** occurs or the receiver's window is reached. This algorithm is called **slow start**.

Assume the maximum segment size is 1KB and the congestion window is 64KB initially. But a timeout occurred. So the threshold is set to 32KB and the congestion window to 1KB for time 0. The congestion window then grows exponentially until it reaches the threshold. From that point (the threshold) on, it grows linearly, which is **congestion avoidance**. Figure 5. 9 illustrates the work process of congestion algorithms.

Fast retransmit is a modification to the congestion avoidance algorithm. The **fast**

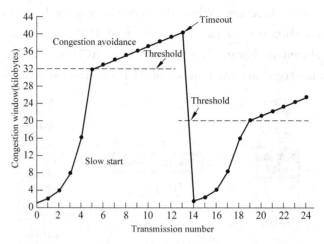

Figure 5.9　An example of the congestion algorithm

retransmit algorithm uses the arrival of 3 duplicate **ACKs** as an indication that a segment has been lost. After receiving 3 duplicate ACKs, TCP performs a **retransmission**, without waiting for the retransmission timer to expire.

When the timeout occurs and **fast recovery** is used to control congestion, the threshold is set to half of the current threshold, and the congestion window to the size of the threshold for next time. Then, the congestion window grows linearly.

Notes

① TCP service is obtained by both the sender and receiver creating end points, called sockets. 在这个句子中 called sockets 省略了主语和谓语,应该是 they are called sockets。

② The *Window size* field tells how many bytes may be sent starting at the byte acknowledged. 在这个句子中 starting at the byte 修饰前面的 bytes,acknowledged 修饰前面直接接的 byte,表示以应答字节开始。

③ The CONNECT primitive sends a TCP segment with the SYN bit on and ACK bit off and waits for a response. 在此句中 with 引导介词短语,修饰前面的 segment。

④ Because of the limitation of network capacity and receiver capacity, congestion appears when the load offered to any network is more than it can handle. 在 when 引导的从句中,the load 是主语 offered to any network 修饰 load,谓语是 is,其后面又接了一个从句,表示超出了可以处理的负载。

New Words and Phrases

reliable	[ri'laiəbl]	*adj.*	可靠的;可信的
stream	[stri:m]	*n.*	(小)河;水流;(人;车;气)流;组
robust	[rəʊ'bʌst]	*adj.*	强健的;稳固的;耐用的
uniquely	[ju'ni:kli]	*adv.*	独特地;唯一地;珍奇地
acknowledgement	[ək'nɔlidʒmənt]	*n.*	承认;确认;感谢

fixed-format	['fikst'fɔːmæt]	adj.	固定格式的
release	[ri'liːs]	vt.	释放
establish	[i'stæbliʃ]	v.	建立;确立;创办;安顿
congestion	[kən'dʒestʃən]	n.	阻塞;拥挤;充血
threshold	['θreʃhəuld]	n.	门槛;开端;界限;入口
exponentially	[ˌekspə'nenʃəli]	adv.	成倍地;幂地;指数地
timeout	[taim'aut]	n.	超时;过期;暂停
retransmission	[riːtrænz'miʃən]	n.	中继;转播;重发

Computer Terminologies

TSAP (Transport Service Access Point)	传输服务接入点
three-way handshake	三次握手
slow start	慢开始
congestion avoidance	拥塞避免
fast retransmit	快速重发
fast recovery	快速恢复

Exercises

Answer the questions.

1. If you want to browse the WWW, then which port should be open?
2. If you want to transfer the files, then which port should be open?
3. What does FIN mean in the TCP segment head?
4. How is the TCP connection established?
5. How is the TCP connection is released?
6. Describe the slow start algorithm.
7. Describe the basic idea of the fast retransmit algorithm.
8. What is the sockets?

Extending Your Reading

Lab: Exploring TCP

In this lab, you'll use the web browser to access a file from a Web server. You will use Ethereal or Sniffer to capture the packets arriving at your computer. You'll also be able to download a packet trace from the Web server from which you download the file. In this server trace, you will find the packets that were generated by your own access of the Web server. You will analysis the client- and server-side traces to explore aspects of TCP. In particular, you will evaluate the performance of the TCP connection between your computer and the Web server. You will trace TCP's window behavior, and infer packet loss, retransmission, flow control and congestion control behavior, and estimated round-trip time.

参考译文

TCP 以及拥塞控制

TCP

　　TCP(传输控制协议)工作在传输层,设计在一个非可信的互联网络上提供一个可靠的端到端的字节流传输。互联网络在拓扑、带宽、延迟、分组大小以及其他参数上可能彼此不相同。TCP 可以动态地适应这些性质,它在面对很多故障时也是强健的。它被正式定义在 RFC 793 文件中。

套接字和端口

　　TCP 向应用层提供服务。TCP 服务通过发送端和接收端创建的端点来获得,此端点也叫做套接字。一个套接字包含了主机的 IP 地址和它的 16 位端口号。一个 TCP 连接由通信的两端唯一标志。也就是说,TCP 连接={套接字 1,套接字 2}={(IP1:端口 1),(IP2:端口 2)}。

　　端口是传输服务接入点的 TCP 名字,用来识别应用层的过程。一般来说,端口可分为三类:

　　熟知的端口:0～1023,为标准服务保留。图 5.5 列出了一些比较熟知的服务。

　　已注册端口:1024～49151,不知名的端口保留给应用程序。

　　客户端端口:49152～65535,保留给客户端过程,占时使用。

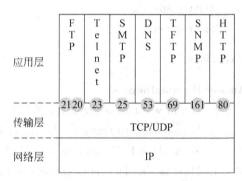

图 5.5　一些已分配端口

TCP 协议

　　TCP 一个重要的特点是 TCP 连接有它自己的 32 位序列号,用来应答和窗口机制。TCP 以数据段的形式交换数据。每个段以一个固定格式 20 字节长度的头开始,如图 5.6 所示。

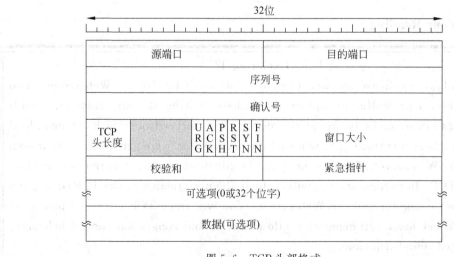

图 5.6　TCP 头部格式

源端口和目的端口字段标志连接的本地端点。

序列号字段是发送数据的编号。

应答编号的字段表明期望的下一字节的编号,不是正确接收的最后一字节。

TCP 头部长度表明有多少个 32 位字包含在 TCP 头部。

接下来是没有被使用的 6 位字段以及 6 个 1 位标志。紧急指针使用,则设置 URG 为 1。ACK 位设置为 1,表示应答序号是合法的。PSH 位表明推进数据。RST 位用来重设变得混乱的连接。FIN 位用来释放连接。它表明发送者已经没有数据发送。

窗口大小字段表明从应答字节开始多少字节被发送。

校验和字段用来提供额外的可靠性。

TCP 连接建立

TCP 连接建立通过在服务器客户端之间建立三次握手方式。首先,服务器通过执行 LISTEN 和 ACCEPT 原语被动等待发送来的连接。然后,客户端执行 CONNECT 原语。CONNECT 原语发送一个保持 SYN 位开、ACK 位关的 TCP 段,接着等待响应。当服务器接收到这个段,它既可以接受连接,也可以拒绝连接。如果它接受,则送回一个应答段。TCP 建立连接的过程一般情况如图 5.7 所示。

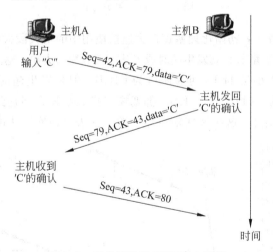

图 5.7　正常情况下 TCP 建立连接

TCP 连接释放

无论是客户端还是服务器都可以发送一个设置了 FIN 位的 TCP 段来释放连接,表示不再有数据发送。当 FIN 被应答,那个方向的数据传输关闭。虽然如此,数据可能无限制地朝另外一个方向流动。当两个方向的传输都已经关闭,则连接被释放。正常地,释放连接需要四个 TCP 段,如图 5.8 所示。如果第一个 ACK 和第二个 FIN 能包含在同一个段里,则 TCP 的段数减少到三。

TCP 拥塞控制

由于网络和接收方性能的限制,当提供给任何网络的负载超过它的处理能力时,拥塞出现了。为了解决这些问题,一些方法提出来了:慢开始、拥塞避免、快速重发以及快恢复。发送者在他们之间保持两个窗口和一个参数:授权的接收窗口、拥塞窗口以及临界值。

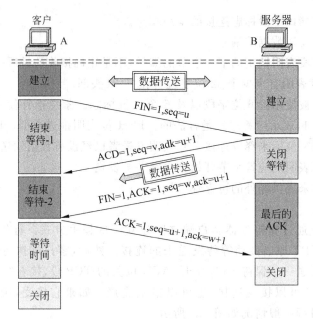

图 5.8　TCP 释放连接

当一个连接建立,发送者初始化拥塞窗口为连接使用中的最大段大小。它然后发送一个最大段。拥塞窗口保持指数增长直到发生超时或者达到接收窗口大小。这个算法叫做慢启动。

假如起初最大段大小是 1KB,拥塞窗口为 64KB。但是发生超时。因此临界值设置为 32KB,拥塞窗口时间为 0 时设置为 1KB。拥塞窗口指数增长直到它到达临界值。从临界点开始,拥塞窗口呈直线增长,这叫做拥塞避免。图 5.9 表示拥塞算法的工作过程。

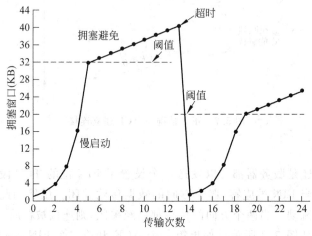

图 5.9　TCP 拥塞控制的一个例子

快速重发是拥塞避免算法的改进。快速重发使用 3 个重复 ACK 的到达表明一个段丢失。在接收了 3 个重复的 ACK 之后,TCP 执行快速重发,无须等待重传计时器到期。

当超时发生,快速恢复用来控制拥塞,临界值设置为目前临界值的一半,拥塞窗口大小设置为下一个时间的临界值。然后,拥塞窗口线形增长。

Unit 6　The Application Layer

Section A　Network Applications

I. Introduction

The applications of computer networks are diverse. Over the past thirty years, people have **conceived** of such networking applications as remote access to computers, electronic mail, file transfers and chat. Recently, multimedia applications appear, such as the World Wide Web, video conferencing, audio and video on demand.

The software is also very important for network applications. Generally, a application of network software is distributed among two or more end systems. For example, with the Web there are two pieces of software that communicate with each other: the browser software in the user's host, and the Web server software in the Web server. With **multiparty** video conferencing, there is a software piece that manages each host to participate in the conference. Next, we will examine four real applications.

II. WWW and HTTP

The World Wide Web (WWW) is an **architectural framework** for accessing linked documents all over the Internet and the Hypertext Transfer Protocol (HTTP) is its application-layer protocol.

1. WWW

From the users' point of view, the Web consists of a vast, worldwide collection of documents or Web pages, often called **pages** for short. Each page may contain links to other pages anywhere in the world. The users can get the page pointed to if they click on a link. This process can be repeated indefinitely. The idea of having one page point to another is called **hypertext**, invented by a visionary M. I. T. professor Vannevar Bush in 1945. Pages are named using **URL** (Uniform Resource Locators), which includes three parts: the protocol, the hostname and the page's path. A typical URL is like http://www.abcd.com/products.html, in which the name of the protocol is http, the hostname is www.abcd.com and products.html is its path.

When a link is selected, some steps are done as follows. Assume that you have clicked on a link http://www.pku.edu.cn/.

- The browser determines the URL.
- The browser asks DNS for the IP address of www.pku.edu.cn.
- DNS replies with 124.205.79.6.
- The browser makes a TCP connection to port 80 on 124.205.79.6.
- It then sends over a request asking for file /home/index.html.
- The www.pku.edu.cn server sends the file /home/index.html.
- The TCP connection is released.
- The browser displays all the text in /home/index.html.
- The browser fetches and displays all images in this file.

The basic web model of how the web works is shown in Figure 6.1.

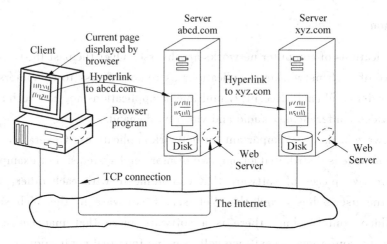

Figure 6.1　Parts of the web model

2. HTTP

HTTP is used throughout the World Wide Web. It specifies what messages clients may send to servers and what responses they get back in return. HTTP is implemented in two programs: a client program and server program. HTTP defines the structure of the messages and how the client and server exchange the messages.

The usual way for a browser to contact a server is to establish a TCP connection as

their underlying transport protocol. ① There are two versions of HTTP: 1.0 and 1.1. In HTTP 1.0, after the connection was established, a single request was sent over and a single response was sent back. Then the TCP connection was released. HTTP 1.1 supports persistent connections. It is possible to send a request and get a response between the client and the server repeatedly by using HTTP 1.1.

III. FTP

FTP (File Transfer Protocol) is a protocol for transferring a file from one host to another host. It dates back to 1971, but remains enormously popular. A typical working mechanism of FTP is shown in Figure 6.2. The user first provides the hostname of the remote host as FTP server and makes the local host to establish a TCP connection with the FTP server by using FTP user agent. If the username and password provided by the user is passed, the user can transfer one or more files stored in the remote server to the local host, or vice versa.

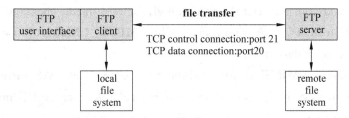

Figure 6.2   FTP moves files between the client and server

FTP uses two parallel TCP connections to transfer a file: a control connection and a data connection. When FTP works, Port 20 and 21 are also used for these connections. First, a user sets up a control TCP connection with a remote FTP server on port 21. The client side of FTP sends user authentication information to request a file transfer. Once the user is authorized, FTP opens a TCP data connection on port 20. FTP sends exactly one file over the data connection and then closes the data connection. If the user wants to transfer another file during the same session, FTP creates a new data connection. But, the control connection of FTP remains open throughout the duration of the session.

IV. E-mail in the Internet

Along with the Web, electronic mail is one of the most popular Internet applications. In contrast with **snail mail**, electronic mail is fast, inexpensive and easy to distribute. Moreover, modern electronic mail includes hyperlinks, images, sound and even video except for text.

1. SMTP

The simple mail transfer protocol (**SMTP**) is the application-layer protocol for Internet electronic mail. It uses the reliable data transfer service of TCP to transfer mail between the client side and the server side. Both the client and server sides of SMTP run on every mail server. When a mail server sends mail, it acts as an SMTP client. When a mail server receives mail, it acts as an SMTP server. The main components of E-mail are shown in Figure 6.3.

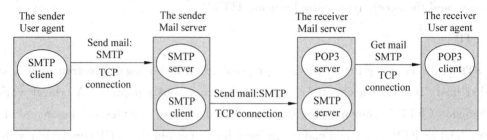

Figure 6.3 The components of E-mail

2. MIME

While the message headers described in RFC 822 are satisfactory for sending ordinary ASCII text, they are not sufficiently rich enough for multimedia messages or for carrying non-ASCII text formats.[2] A solution, called **MIME** (Multipurpose Internet Mail Extensions), is now widely used.

The basic idea of MIME is to continue to use the RFC 822 format, but to add structure to the message body and define encoding rules for non-ASCII messages. MIME messages can be sent using the existing mail programs and protocols.

3. Mail Access Protocols

Currently, there are two popular mail access protocols: **POP**3 (Post Office Protocol - Version 3) and **IMAP** (Internet Mail Access Protocol). Both are used to transfer mail from the recipient's mail server to the recipient's user agent. POP3 is an extremely simple mail access protocol and has limited functionality. It uses a TCP connection to the mail server on port 110 when it works. IMAP is designed to allow users to manipulate remote mailboxes as if they were local. It has commands that permit a user agent to obtain components of messages.

V. DNS

The **DNS** (Domain Name System) is a distributed database implemented in a hierarchy of **name servers**, and is an application-layer protocol that maps host names to IP addresses.

1. How does DNS Work?

The essence of DNS is a hierarchical, domain-based naming scheme. The work way of DNS is as follows. To map a name onto an IP address, an application program calls a library procedure called the resolver. The resolver sends a UDP packet to a local DNS server, which then looks up the name and returns the IP address to the **resolver**, then returns it to the caller. After getting the IP address, the program can then establish a TCP connection with the destination or send it UDP packets.

2. The DNS Name Space

Conceptually，the Internet is divided into over 200 top-level domains，where each domain covers many hosts. Each domain is partitioned into sub-domains，and these are further partitioned，and so on. All these domains can be represented by a tree.

Notes

① The usual way for a browser to contact a server is to establish a TCP connection as their underlying transport protocol. 在本句话中主语是 way，a browser to contact a server 修饰其前面的名词 way，as their underlying transport protocol 修饰其前面的 connection。

② While the message headers described in RFC 822 are satisfactory for sending ordinary ASCII text，they are not sufficiently rich enough for multimedia messages or for carrying non-ASCII text formats. 在本句话中，described in RFC 822 动词的被动语态做形容词修饰其前面的 message headers，for carrying non-ASCII text formats 介词 for 后面接名词或者动名词。

New Words and Phrases

conceive	[kən'siːv]	v.	设想；想出；怀孕
multiparty	[ˌmʌlti'pɑːti]	adj.	多党的；多方的
architectural	[ˌɑːki'tektʃərəl]	adj.	建筑的；建筑学的
framework	['freimwɜːk]	n.	框架；体系；结构
underlying	[ˌʌndə'laiiŋ]	adj.	潜在的；隐含的；在下面的

Computer Terminologies

pages	网页
Hypertext	超文本
URL（Uniform Resource Locators）	统一资源定位器
FTP（File Transfer Protocol）	文件传输协议
snail mail	"蜗牛"邮递；邮局
SMTP（simple mail transfer protocol）	简单邮件传输协议
MIME（Multipurpose Internet Mail Extensions）	多用途互联网邮件扩展
POP3（Post Office Protocol-Version 3）	邮件协议-第三版
IMAP（Internet Mail Access Protocol）	互联网邮件访问协议
DNS（Domain Name System）	域名系统
name servers	名字服务器
resolver	解析器

Exercises

Translate the sentences into Chinese.

1. Over the past thirty years, people have conceived of such networking applications as remote access to computers, electronic mail, file transfers and chat.

2. The World Wide Web (WWW) is an architectural framework for accessing linked documents all over the Internet and the Hypertext Transfer Protocol (HTTP) is its application-layer protocol.

3. Pages are named using URL (Uniform Resource Locators), which includes three parts: the protocol, the hostname and the page's path.

4. The usual way for a browser to contact a server is to establish a TCP connection as their underlying transport protocol.

5. FTP (File Transfer Protocol) is a protocol for transferring a file from one host to another host.

6. The user first provides the hostname of the remote host as FTP server and makes the local host to establish a TCP connection with the FTP server by using FTP user agent.

7. It uses the reliable data transfer service of TCP to transfer mail between the client side and the server side. Both the client and server sides of SMTP run on mail server.

8. The basic idea of MIME is to continue to use the RFC 822 format, but to add structure to the message body and define encoding rules for non-ASCII messages.

9. Currently, there are two popular mail access protocols: **POP**3 (Post Office Protocol-Version 3) and **IMAP** (Internet Mail Access Protocol).

Extending Your Reading

Case history—Hotmail

In 1995, the Internet venture capitalist Draper Fisher Jurvetson developed a free Web-based e-mail system. The idea was to give a free-email account to anyone who wanted one, and to make the accounts accessible from the Web. Anyone with a Web-based E-mail could read and send E-mail from a school or community library by accessing to the Web. Furthermore, Web-based e-mail would offer great mobility to its subscribers. Then, the company Hotmail was formed, which provided the service of E-mail for subscribers. The number of subscribers grew rapidly, with all of their subscribers being exposed to advertising banners while reading their E-mail. In December 1997, less than 18 months after launching the service, Hotmail had over 12 million subscribers and was acquired by Microsoft, reportedly for $400 million dollars.

参考译文

网　络　应　用

计算机网络应用各种各样。在过去的三十年里，人们已经设想到像远程连接计算机、电子邮件、文件传输以及聊天这样的网络应用程序。近来，多媒体应用出现了，如万维网、视频会议、音频和视频点播。

软件也是很重要的网络应用。一般地，一个网络应用软件分布在两台或者多台终端系统上。比如，在万维网中，软件有两部分程序彼此通信，分别是用户主机上的浏览器软件和Web服务器上的Web服务器软件。对于多方视频会议，软件有一个模块管理参与会议的每一个主机。接下来将要考察四个实际的应用。

WWW 和 HTTP

WWW是在 Internet 上获取连接文档的体系框架，HTTP是它的应用层协议。

WWW

从用户的观点，WWW包含了大量的、世界范围的文档或者是网页，经常简称为页面的集合。每一个页面可能包含了到世界上任何地方的其他页面的链接。如果用户点击链接，则用户可以获得被点击的页面。这个过程可以无限制重复。一个页面指向另一个页面的思想叫做超文本，它是一个有远见的麻省理工学院的教授 Vannevar Bush 于 1945 年发明的。页面使用 URL(统一资源定位器)命名，它包含三个部分：协议、主机名、网页路径。典型的URL 像 http://www.abcd.com/products.html，在这个网址里 HTTP 是协议，主机名是www.abcd.com，products.html 是路径。

当选择一个链接，将完成如下一些步骤。假设单击了链接 http://www.pku.edu.cn/。

- 浏览器确定 URL 地址。
- 浏览器询问 DNS www.pku.edu.cn 的 IP 地址。
- DNS 回复 124.205.79.6。
- 浏览器建立一个到 124.205.79.6 主机上 80 端口的连接。
- 它发送一个获取文件/home/index.html 的请求。
- www.pku.edu.cn 服务器发送文件/home/index.html。
- TCP 连接释放。
- 浏览器显示/home/index.html 中的所有的文本。
- 浏览器获取并显示文件上的所有图片。

WWW 工作的基本模型如图 6.1 所示。

HTTP

HTTP 贯穿了整个 WWW。它规定了客户端可以发送什么信息给服务器，客户端可以获得什么应答。HTTP 由两个程序来实现：一个客户端程序，一个服务器端程序。HTTP定义了信息的结构以及客户和服务器之间如何交流信息。

浏览器连接服务器的通常方式是建立 TCP 连接，作为其下层的传输协议。HTTP 有两个版本：1.0 和 1.1，在连接建立之后，发送一个请求，返回一个应答，然后 TCP 连接被释

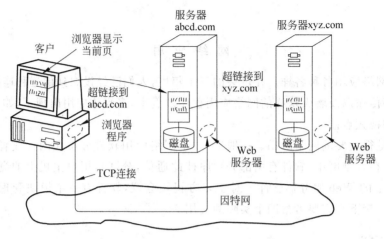

图 6.1　部分 Web 模型

放。HTTP 1.1 支持持久性连接。通过使用 HTTP 1.1 它能够在客户服务器之间重复地发送一个请求并获得一个应答。

FTP

FTP 是一种从一台主机传输文件到另一台主机的文件传输协议。它起源于 1971 年，但仍然广泛流行。FTP 典型的工作机制如图 6.2 所示。用户首先提供作为 FTP 服务器的远程主机名，通过使用 FTP 用户代理建立一个从本地主机到 FTP 服务器的 TCP 连接。如果用户提供的用户名和密码通过了，那么用户就可以从远程主机上传输一个或者多个文件到本地主机，反之亦然。

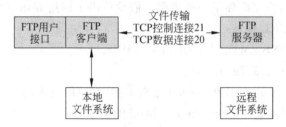

图 6.2　FTP 在客户-服务器之间传输文件

FTP 使用两个并行的 TCP 连接传输文件：一个控制连接，一个数据连接。当 FTP 工作时，端口 20 和端口 21 用于这些连接。首先，一个用户设置一个同远程 FTP 服务器端口 21 的 TCP 控制连接。FTP 的客户端发送一个用户验证信息要求文件传输。一旦用户被授权，FTP 在端口 20 上打开一个 TCP 数据连接。FTP 在数据连接上只发送一个文件，然后关闭数据连接。如果用户想要在同一个会话上传输另外一个文件，FTP 创建一个新的数据连接。但是，FTP 的控制连接在整个会话期间一直保持打开状态。

因特网上的 E-mail

随着 WWW 的发展，电子邮件是 Internet 最流行应用之一。与邮局信件相比，电子邮件的速度非常快,便宜且容易发布。此外,现代的电子邮件包括除了文字之外有超级链接、图片、声音、视频。

SMTP

　　SMTP 是 Internet 电子邮件的应用层协议。它使用 TCP 的可信的数据传输服务在客户和服务器之间传输邮件。无论是 SMTP 的客户端还是服务器端都运行在邮件服务器上。当邮件服务器发送邮件,它作为 SMTP 客户端。当一个邮件服务器接收邮件,它作为 SMTP 的服务器。E-mail 的主要组成部分如图 6.3 所示。

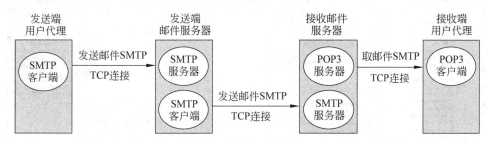

图 6.3　E-mail 组成

MIME

　　当 RFC 822 中描述的信息头部满足发送普通 ASCII 文本时,它们不能充分满足发送多媒体信息或者非 ASCII 文本格式。一个叫做 MIME 的解决方案广泛被使用。

　　MIME 的基本思想是持续使用 RFC 822 的格式,但是在信息体增加了一个结构,并为非 ASCII 信息定义了编码规则。MIME 信息可以通过使用存在的邮件程序和协议发送。

邮件接入协议

　　目前,有两个流行的邮件接入协议: POP3 和 IMAP。两者都是用来从接收者的邮件服务器传输邮件到接收者的代理。POP3 是一个非常简单的邮件接入协议,功能有限。当工作时,它使用 TCP 连接到邮件服务器的 110 端口。IMAP 设计用来允许用户像操作本地邮箱一样地操作远程邮箱。它有允许用户代理获得信息组件的命令。

DNS

　　DNS 是实现了命名服务器多层结构的分布式数据库,是一个主机名到 IP 地址映射的应用层协议。

DNS 是如何工作的

　　DNS 的本质是一个层次的、基于域名的命名模式。DNS 的工作方式如下。应用程序调用叫做解析器的库程序实现名字到 IP 地址的映射。解析器发送 UDP 分组到本地 DNS 服务器,它寻找名字并返回其 IP 地址给解析器,然后返回给调用程序。在获得了 IP 地址之后,然后程序建立一个带有目的的 TCP 连接或者发送 UDP 分组给它。

DNS 命名空间

　　从概念上来说,Internet 被划分为 200 多级域名,每一级覆盖了很多的主机。每一个域名划分为多个子域名,子域名又被进一步划分,等等。所有的这些域名可以表示成一棵树。

Section B　Network Software

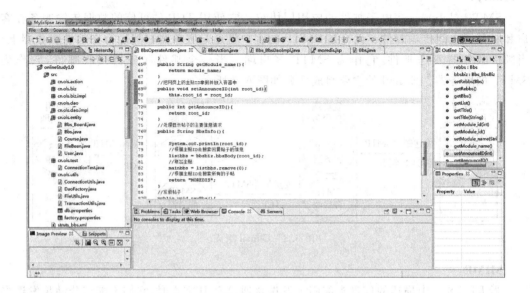

I. Introduction

The computer network is a collection of autonomous computers interconnected by a technology and is a complicated system. Generally, the network software is used to analysis and research computer networks. Such software can be divided into three types: network development tools, network **simulation** tools and network analysis tools. The popular development tools for computer networks are the Java programming language, the HyperText Markup Language (HTML), **XML (eXtensible Markup Language)**, PHP, JSP, ASP. net and so on. NS2, **OMNeT ++** [①], **OPNET**[②] are used to simulate the wired or wireless network in order to analysis the performance of the network. The capture software, such as **Sniffer**[③] and **Wireshark**[④], normally combined with the simulation tool **Packet Tracer**[⑤] or **GNS**3[⑥], is also used to analysis network protocols and **diagnose** the network fault.

II. OMNeT ++ simulator

1. What is OMNeT ++ ?

OMNeT ++ (Objective Modular Network Test-bed in C ++) is an object-oriented modular **discrete** event network simulator. It is a **public-source, component-based**, modular and open-architecture simulation environment with strong GUI support and an embeddable simulation kernel. OMNeT++ provides a component-architecture for models. Components (modules) are programmed in C ++, then, **assembled** into larger components and models using a high-level language (NED). OMNeT ++ is free for academic and non-profit use, but commercial users must obtain a license from Omnest Global Inc.

OMNeT ++ model consists of simple modules and compound modules, as shown in Figure 6.4. Simple modules are atomic elements in the module hierarchy, which can not be divided any further. Messages can be sent either via output gates or directly to another module. Gates are the input and output interfaces of modules linked with connections. Compound module is consists of simple modules, and its hierarchy level is unlimited. The Node in WSN is compound modules, which consists of simple modules: Application module, Coordinator modules, Energy module and Sensor module. This structure is defined by NED (NEtwork Description) language. NED is the topology description language of OMNeT ++, and can be edited by both the text and graphical user interface (GUI). The graphical user interface is shown in Figure 6.5.

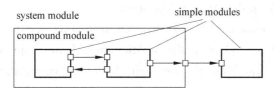

Figure 6.4   Model structure in OMNeT ++

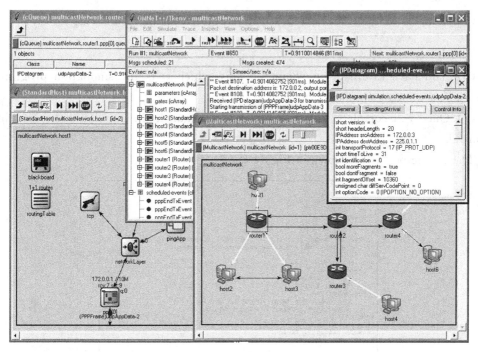

Figure 6.5   Graphical user interface

2. Installation

OMNeT ++ can run well on operating system of Linux, Win32 platforms or most other UNIX-like systems. The third party software used in OMNeT ++ includes C++

compiler，Tcl/Tk，Perl，and so on. Now we give steps of install OMNeT++ on Windows with the Cygwin platform.

The install steps：

(1) Install Cygwin；

(2) Install OMNeT++；

(3) Add omnetpp/bin to the PATH；

(4) Make sure nedtool，gned，opp_makemake and the sample simulations work.

3. TicToc Tutorial for OMNeT++

This short **tutorial** to OMNeT++ guides you through an example of modeling and simulation，showing you along the way some of the commonly used OMNeT++ features. The steps for tictoc' application is as follows：

(1) Create a working directory called tictoc.

(2) Describe your example network by creating a topology file(* . ned).

(3) We now need to implement the functionality of the simple module(* . cc).

(4) We now create the Makefile which will help us to compile and link our program to create the executable tictoc：

```
$ opp_makemake
```

(5) Compile and link our very first simulation by making command：

```
$ make
```

(6) You have to create one omnetpp. ini，which tells the simulation program the network you want to simulate.

(7) Once you complete the above steps，you launch the simulation by issuing the command.

The file tictoc. ned is shown in Figure 6. 6.

```
simple Txc1
    gates:
        in: in;
        out: out;
endsimple

//
// Two instances (tic and toc) of Txc1 connected both ways.
// Tic and toc will pass messages to one another.
//
module Tictoc1
    submodules:
        tic: Txc1;
        toc: Txc1;
    connections:
        tic.out --> delay 100ms --> toc.in;
        tic.in <-- delay 100ms <-- toc.out;
endmodule

network tictoc1 : Tictoc1
endnetwork
```

Figure 6. 6   tictoc. ned

4. Visualizing the results with Plove and Scalars

The Plove is a handy tool for **plotting** and analyzing OMNeT++ simulation results. It works with output **vector** files. Output vector files contain several output vectors，one of which contains a time series: several values with **timestamps**. Plove can plot output vectors, one or more in a graph. You can specify the drawing style (lines, dots etc) for each vector. You can set axis bounds, scaling, titles and labels, etc. You can save the graphs to files in various formats (EPS, GIF, etc) or copy them to the clipboard. Figure 6.7 is an example of visualizing the results with Plove.

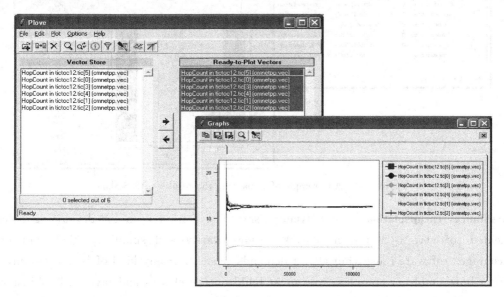

Figure 6.7   An example of visualizing the results with Plove

The Scalars is a handy tool for creating bar charts and x-y plots from OMNeT++ output **scalar** files (omnetpp. sca by default). You can save the graphs to files in various formats (EPS, GIF, etc) or copy them to the clipboard. Figure 6.8 gives an example of visualizing the results with the Scalars.

III. Java Language

The Java language is a programming language, which has a vocabulary, grammar and **syntax**. A Java program is executed in a form of a sequence of instruments that can be run by a computer. It builds on the familiar and useful features of C++ while removing the complex and **superfluous** elements, so that is safer, simpler and easier to use.

1. Java is Object-Oriented

Java deals with classes and objects. They are the basis for the entire programming language rather than more data structures that are available to the programmer.

In C++, you can declare a class, a structure or a union, and use them in style of C language. In Java, classes and objects are the center of the language, and everything else is resolved around them. You can't use *structures*, *unions*, or *typedefs* because they have gone. You either use classes and objects. It's simple.

Java provides all the luxuries of **object-oriented** programming: class hierarchy,

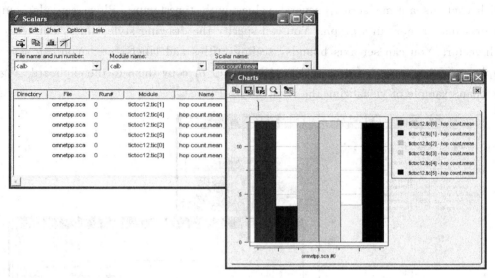

Figure 6.8　An example of visualizing the results with Scalars

inheritance，encapsulation，and **polymorphism.** The main reason for developing object-oriented software is reuse of objects besides clarity and simplicity. Java not only encourages software reuse，but also it demands reuse. For any kind of Java program，no matter how simple or complex，you must build on the classes and Java API. When you begin to develop software in Java，you may build on the classes you have developed and reuse them.

2. Java is Multithreaded

Java provides build-in language support for **multithreading.** Multithreading allows more than one thread of execution to take place within a single program，which make a program do many things at the same time. It also allows Java to use **idle** CPU time to perform the necessary **garbage** collection and general system maintenance with less impact on program performance.

Writing multithreaded programs is like dating several people concurrently. Everything works well until threads interact with each other with unexpected ways. Java provides multithreading working safely and correctly by providing **synchronization** capacities.

3. Java is Interpreted and Portable

While it is true that the **compile code** is run quickly，it is also true that the **interpreted code** can usually be developed and fielded more quickly in a more flexible manner. It is also much more portable.

Java must be interpreted in order to be a truly **platform-independent** programming language. It does not run as fast as compiled native code，and the work is underway to translate Java byte-code into machine code as it is loaded.

The advantage of being interpreted outweighs any performance impacts. If an operating system runs the Java interpreter and supports the Java API，it can run all Java programs. The interpreted program is much more easily updated. The recompilation of Java programs is done automatically. Besides the Java's interpreted feature, linking is also powerful and flexible. The system of running Java programs supports dynamic linking between local class files and those that are downloaded from the Internet.

4. Java is a programming language of the Web

Java has become the **de facto** programming language of the web. It is being **licensed** by the software company, and is a most powerful language for developing platform-independent software.

Java is also evolving beyond the web and becoming a key component in distribute application development. Some **releases** of Sun's products emphasize Java's importance to distributed object-oriented software development.

Notes

① OMNeT++ 基于离散事件(仿真),是一个免费的、开源的多协议网络仿真软件。OMNeT++ 英文全称是 Objective Modular Network Testbed in C++,是近年来在科学和工业领域逐渐流行的一种基于组件的模块化开放网络仿真平台。

② OPNET 是一个网络仿真技术软件包,它能够准确分析复杂网络的性能和行为,在网络模型中的任意位置都可以插入标准的或用户指定的探头,以采集数据和进行统计。

③ Sniffer 是一种基于被动侦听原理的网络分析软件。使用这种技术,可以监视网络的状态、数据流动情况以及网络上传输的信息。

④ Wireshark 是一个网络数据包分析软件,其功能是截取网络数据包,并尽可能显示出最为详细的网络数据包数据。

⑤ Packet Tracer 是由 Cisco 公司发布的一个辅助学习工具,为学习 Cisco 网络课程的初学者设计、配置网络和排除网络故障提供了网络模拟环境。用户可以在软件的图形用户界面上直接使用拖曳方法建立网络拓扑,并可提供数据包在网络中进行的详细处理过程,观察网络实时运行情况。

⑥ GNS3 是一款优秀的具有图形化界面可以运行在多平台(如 Windows、Linux 和 MacOS 等)的网络仿真软件。Cisco 网络设备管理员或是想要通过 CCNA、CCNP、CCIE 等 Cisco 认证考试的相关人士可以通过它来完成相关的实验模拟操作。同时它也可以用于虚拟体验 Cisco 网际操作系统 IOS 或者是检验将要在真实的路由器上部署实施的相关配置。简单地说,GNS3 是 **Dynamips** 的一个图形前端,相比直接使用 Dynamips 这样的虚拟软件要更容易上手和更具有可操作性。

New Words and Phrases

simulation	[ˌsimjuˈleiʃn]	n.	模仿,模拟
diagnose	[ˈdaiəgnəʊz]	vt.	诊断;判断
syntax	[ˈsintæks]	n.	句法;语构;语法
superfluous	[suːˈpɜːfluəs]	adj.	多余的;不必要的;奢侈的
inheritance	[inˈheritəns]	n.	继承;遗传;遗产

encapsulation	[inˌkæpsjuˈleʃən]	n.	包装；封装；包裹
polymorphism	[ˌpɔliˈmɔːfizəm]	n.	多型现象；多态性
multithread	[məltiθˈred]	n.	多线程；多流
idle	[ˈaidl]	adj.	空闲的；懒惰的；无根据的
garbage	[ˈgɑːbidʒ]	n.	垃圾；脏东西
synchronization	[ˌsiŋkrənaiˈzeiʃn]	n.	同一时刻；同步；同时性
de facto	[ˌdeiˈfæktəʊ]	adj.	＜拉＞实际的；事实上的
license	[ˈlaisəns]	vt.	同意；发许可证
release	[riˈliːs]	vt.	释放；放开；发布；发行
discrete	[diˈskriːt]	adj.	分离的；不相关联的；非连续
assemble	[əˈsembl]	vt.	装配；组合
tutorial	[tjuːˈtɔːriəl]	n.	教程；使用说明书
plot	[plɔt]	vt.	以图表画出；制图
vector	[ˈvektə]	n.	矢量；航向
timestamp	[ˈtaimstæmp]	n.	时间戳
scalar	[ˈskeilə]	n.	数量；标量

Computer Terminologies

XML (eXtensible Markup Language)	可扩展的标记语言
object-oriented	面向对象
compile code	编译代码
interpreted code	解释代码
platform-independent	跨平台
public-source	公开源代码
component-based	基于组件

Exercises

I. Answer the questions.

1. Describe the types of network software.

2. What is OMNeT++ ?

3. Describe the steps of installing OMNeT++ .

4. Describe the steps of tictoc simulation applications.

5. Describe the use of the tool Plove.

II. Fill in the blanks with these words *plotting*，*component-based*，*inheritance*，*multithreading*，*object-oriented*，*simulator*，*XML*，*simulation*.

1. Such software can be divided into three types：network development tools，network (   ) tools and network analysis tools.

2. The popular development tools for computer networks are the Java programming language，the HyperText Markup Language (HTML)，(   )，PHP，JSP，ASP.net and

so on.

3. OMNeT++ (Objective Modular Network Test-bed in C++) is an object-oriented modular discrete event network (　　).

4. The Plove is a handy tool for (　　) and analyzing OMNeT++ simulation results.

5. Java provides all the luxuries of (　　) programming：class hierarchy, (　　), encapsulation, and polymorphism.

6. Java provides build-in language support for (　　).

7. It is a public-source, (　　), modular and open-architecture simulation environment with strong GUI support and an embeddable simulation kernel.

Extending Your Reading

Principles in practice—DNS

　　Like HTTP, FTP, and SMTP, the DNS protocol is an application-layer protocol. The reason is that：(1) it runs between communicating end systems using the client-server paradigm, (2) it relies on an underlying end-to-end transport protocol to transfer DNS messages between communicating end systems. In another sense, however, the role of the DNS is quite different from Web, file transfer and e-mail application. Unlike these applications, the DNS is not an application with which a user directly interacts. Instead, the DNS provides a core Internet function—namely, translating hostnames to their underlying IP addresses, for user applications and other software in the Internet. The DNS implements the critical name-to-address translation process using clients and servers located at the edge of the network.

参考译文

网 络 软 件

引言

　　计算机网络是一组有自治能力的计算机,它们由一种技术相互连接组合起来,是一个复杂的系统。一般来说,网络软件用来分析和研究计算机网络。这些软件可以分为三类:网络开发工具、网络模拟工具、网络分析工具。流行的计算机网络开发工具是 Java 程序设计语言、HTML、XML、PHP、JSP、ASP. NET 等。NS2、OMNeT++、OPNET 用来仿真有线和无线网络分析网络的性能。捕捉软件如 Sniffer、Wireshark 一般与仿真工具 Packet Tracer、GNS3 相结合用来分析网络协议和诊断网络问题。

OMNeT++ 模拟器

什么是 OMNeT++ 模拟器?

　　OMNeT++(C++ 中的目标模块化网络测试床)是一个面向对象模块化的离散事件网络模拟器。它是一个公开源代码、基于组件、模块化的带有超强图形用户界面支持和嵌套仿真内核的开放架构的模拟环境。OMNeT++提供一个组件架构模型。模块都用C++编程，然后使用更高一级的语言组合成更大的组件和模型。OMNeT++是学术自由以及非赢利的，但是商业用户必须从Omnest全球公司获得一个许可证。

OMNeT++模型由简单模块和复合模块组成，如图6.4所示。简单模块在模块层次中是原子元素，它不能再分。信息可以通过出口发送出去或者直接传送给另一个模块。出口是模块输入与输出的模型连接接口。复合模块由简单模块组成，它的层次结构是无限制的。无线传感器网络中的节点是复合模块，它由简单模块组成：应用模块、调节模块、能源模块、感应器模块。这个结构是由网络描述语言定义的。网络描述语言是OMNeT++拓扑描述语言，能够被图形用户接口和文字编译。图形用户接口如图6.5所示。

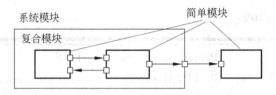

图6.4　OMNeT++模型结构

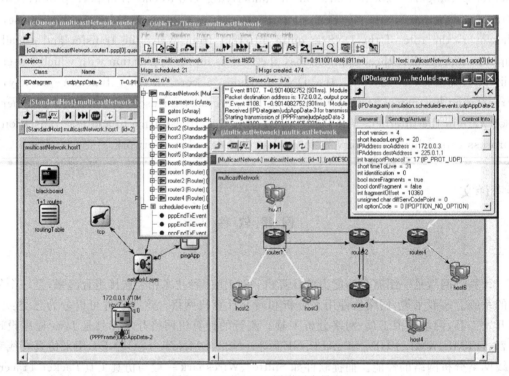

图6.5　OMNeT++图形用户界面

安装

OMNeT++可以很好地运行在Linux操作系统、Win32平台或者许多的其他的类UNIX系统。在OMNeT++中使用的第三方软件包括C++编译器、Tcl/Tk、Perl等。下面给出在Windows的Cygwin平台上安装OMNeT++的步骤：

（1）安装 Cygwin。

（2）安装 OMNeT++。

（3）增加 omnetpp/bin 到路径中。

（4）确保 nedtool、gned、opp-vmake 和实例仿真能工作。

OMNeT++ 的 TicToc 教程

OMNeT++ 的简短教程通过一个模型和防真的例子给出指导，展示 OMNeT++ 经常使用的特性。TicToc 的应用如下：

（1）创建一个叫做 tictoc 的工作路径。

（2）通过创建一个拓扑文件（*.ned）描述一个网络例子。

（3）需要实现简单模块（*.cc）的功能。

（4）需要创建 Makefile，它将帮助我们编译和链接程序，创建可执行的 tictoc：

```
$ opp_makemake
```

（5）通过 make 命令编译和链接第一个仿真程序：

```
$ make
```

（6）必须创建一个 omnetpp.ini，它告诉仿真程序你要模拟的网络。

（7）一旦完成了以上的步骤，可以通过命令发布仿真程序。

Tictoc.ned 文件如图 6.6 所示。

```
simple Txc1
    gates:
        in: in;
        out: out;
endsimple

//
// Two instances (tic and toc) of Txc1 connected both ways.
// Tic and toc will pass messages to one another.
//
module Tictoc1
    submodules:
        tic: Txc1;
        toc: Txc1;
    connections:
        tic.out --> delay 100ms --> toc.in;
        tic.in <-- delay 100ms <-- toc.out;
endmodule

network tictoc1 : Tictoc1
endnetwork
```

图 6.6　tictoc.ned

采用 Plove 和 Scalars 可视化结果

Plove 是一个方便的工具用来绘图和分析 OMNeT++ 模拟结果。它处理输出向量文件。输出向量文件包含几个输出向量，其中一个包含一个时间系列：几个带有时间戳的值。Plove 可以绘出图片中一个或者多个输出向量。为每一个向量可以定置绘画模式（点、线等）。可以设置坐标界限、范围、标题、标记等。可以保存图片各种各样的格式（EPS、GIF等）或者可以将它们保存在剪贴板上。图 6.7 是一个采用 Plove 可视化结果的例子。

Scalars 是一个利用从 OMNeT++ 中输出的标量文件（默认是 omnetpp.sca）用于创建条形图的很方便的工具。可以把图片保存为各种形式的文件（EPS、GIF 等），或者复制到剪贴板中。图 6.8 给出了一个采用 Scalars 可视化结果的例子。

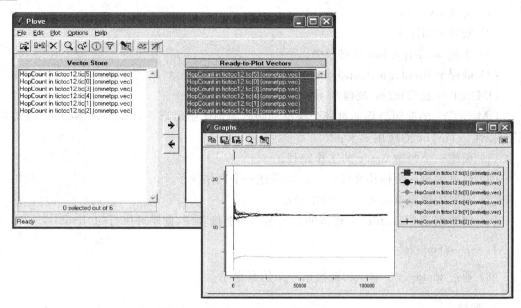

图 6.7 用 Plove 可视化结果的一个例子

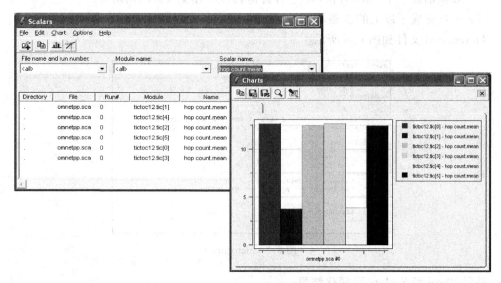

图 6.8 用 Scalars 可视化结果的一个例子

Java 语言

Java 语言是程序设计语言,它有词汇、语法、句法。Java 程序以指令序列的形式执行,能在计算机上运行。它以大家熟知的 C++ 的优点为基础,去除了复杂的多余的元素,因此 Java 语言更加安全、更加简单、容易使用。

Java 是面向对象的

Java 处理类和对象。它们是整个程序设计语言的基础,而不是给程序员呈现更多的数据结构。

在 C++ 中,可以声明一个类、结构、联合,以 C 语言的方式使用它。在 Java 语言中,类和对象是语言的中心,其他的所有一切都围绕它们来执行。你不能使用结构、联合以及类型,因为它们不存在。在 Java 中,既可以使用类又可以使用对象,很简单。

Java 提供所有的面向对象语言的优点:类层次结构、继承、封装、多态性。开发面向对象软件的主要理由除了简单和明了之外就是对象的使用。Java 不只是包括软件复用,但是它要求重用。对于任何一个 Java 程序,无论多么简单或复杂,都必须建立在类和 Java 应用编程接口上。当采用 Java 开发软件时,你可能会建立在你开发的类之上,并重用类。

Java 是多线程

Java 提供了多线程的语言支持。多线程允许在一个单一的程序中存在多个线程的执行,这使得一个程序可在同一时间做很多事情。在对程序性能及少的影响下,它也允许 Java 使用闲散的 CPU 时间执行必要的垃圾回收以及一般的系统维护。

编写多线程程序就像和几个人同时约会一样。一切都工作得很好,直到线程以想不到的方式相互交互。Java 通过提供同步能力提供多线程工作的安全性和正确性。

Java 是解释性的、便携的

实际情况确实是编译代码运行很快。通常可以开发解释代码,它以更灵活的形式运行更换,这是事实。它也更便携。

Java 为了成为真正的平台独立性开发语言必须被解释执行。它的运行没有运行编译好的本地代码速度快。当加载时 Java 程序时,Java 字节码转换成机器码在后台运行。

解释执行的优点多于性能的优化。如果一个操作系统运行 Java 解释器、支持 Java API,它就能运行所有的 Java 程序。解释程序更容易更新。Java 程序的重编译是自动完成的。除了 Java 的解释特点之外,链接是强有力的和灵活的。运行 Java 程序的系统支持本地类文件与从 Internet 上下载的类文件之间的动态链接。

Java 是 Web 程序开发语言

Java 已经成为事实上的 Web 编程语言。它由软件公司授权,是一个开发平台独立软件的强有力语言。

Java 也是涉及除 Web 之外在分布式应用开发中一个关键组成部分。一些 Sun 的产品的发布强调了 Java 对于分布式面向对象软件开发的重要性。

Unit 7　Network Security

Network Security

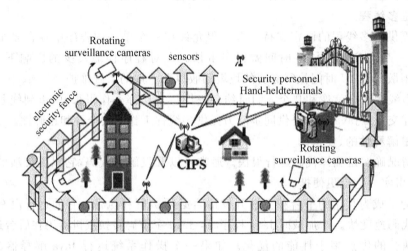

I. Introduction

As millions of people are using networks for communications, shopping, banking, and online offices, network security becomes more and more important. Most security problems are **intentionally** caused by **malicious** people trying to gain some benefit, get attention, or to harm someone. Figure 7.1 list some kinds of people who cause the network security problems.

Adversary	Goal
Student	To have fun snooping on people's E-mail
Cracker	To test out someone's security system;steal data
Sales rep	To claim to represent all of Europe,not just Andorra
Businessman	To discover a competitor's strategic marketing plan
Ex-employee	To get revenge for being fired
Accountant	To embezzle money from a company
Stockbroker	To deny a promise made to a customer by E-mail
Con man	To steal credit card numbers for sale
Spy	To learn an enemy's military or industrial secrets
Terrorist	To steal germ warfare secrets

Figure 7.1　Some perpetrators causing security problems

Network security problems can be divided roughly into three aspects: **secrecy**,

authentication, message **integrity**. Secrecy, also called **confidentiality**, has to do with keeping information out of the hands of unauthorized users. Authentication deals with determining whom you are talking to before revealing **sensitive** information or entering into a business deal. Both the sender and receiver need to confirm the identity of other party involved in the communication. ① Even if the sender and receiver are able to authenticate each other, it is necessary to insure that the content of their communication is not altered in transmission. That is to say, the integrity of messages should be maintained.

Can a "real world" network **intruder** really listen to and record network messages? The answer is "YES". For example, the packet-capturing software **Sniffer** is used to receive passively all frames passing by the network interface of device. **Cryptography** is commonly used to insure secure communications.

II. Cryptography

Cryptography has a long history dating back to Julius Caesar, modern cryptographic techniques used in the Internet are based on it. ② Cryptographic techniques allow a sender to disguise data so that an intruder can gain no information from the intercepted data. The receiver, of course, must be able to recover the original data from the disguised data.

Figure 7.2 shows the encryption model, including some important terminologies. **A cipher** is a character-for-character or bit-for-bit transformation, without regard to the linguistic structure of the message. **A code** replaces one word with another word or symbol. The message to be encrypted is known as the **plaintext**. The output of the encryption process is called the **cipher-text**. The plaintext is often transformed into cipher-text by a function with a **key**. We will use $C = E_K(P)$ to mean that the encryption of the plaintext P using key K gives the cipher-text C. Similarly, $P = D_K(C)$ represents the decryption of C to get the plaintext P.

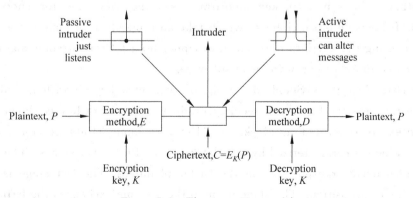

Figure 7.2　The encryption model

The traditional encryption methods have been divided into two categories: **substitution ciphers** and **transposition ciphers**. Now let's look at them briefly.

1. Substitution Ciphers

In a substitution cipher, each letter or group of letters is replaced by another letter or group of letters to **disguise** it. The **Caesar cipher** is the oldest known ciphers, in which. In this method, a becomes D, b becomes E, ..., and z becomes C. For example, the Caesar cipher of "apple" becomes "DSSOH".

2. Transposition Ciphers

Substitution ciphers preserve the order of the plaintext symbols but disguise them. In contrast, transposition ciphers reorder the letters but do not disguise them. The plaintext is written in rows, padded to fill the matrix if need be. The cipher-text is read out by columns, starting with the column whose key letter is the lowest. An example of the transition cipher is given in Figure 7.3.

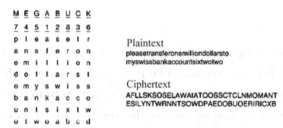

Figure 7.3   A transposition cipher

III. The symmetric-key algorithm

Generally, the traditional **encryption** algorithms are simple. Nowadays, people make the encryption algorithm so complex that the **cryptanalyst** will not be able to make any sense of it without key even if he acquires a large number of enciphered texts. There are two kinds of encryption algorithms typically: the **symmetric-key algorithm** and the **public-key algorithm**. The symmetric-key algorithm uses the same key for encryption and **decryption**. It focus on block ciphers, which take an n-bit block of plaintext as input and transform it using the key into n-bit block of cipher-text.[③] Cryptographic algorithms can be implemented in either hardware or in software.

DES (Data Encryption Standard) is one of symmetric-key algorithms and is widely adopted by the industry for use in security products. The workflow is shown in Figure 7.4. Plaintext is encrypted in blocks of 64bits, yielding 64bits of cipher-text. The algorithm, which is parameterized by a 56-bit key, has 19 distinct stages. The first stage is a key-independent transposition on the 64-bit plaintext. The last stage is the exact **inverse** of this transposition. The stage prior to the last one exchanges the **leftmost** 32bits with the rightmost 32bits. The remaining 16 stages are functionally **identical** but are parameterized by different functions of the key. The algorithm has been designed to allow decryption to be done with the same key as encryption.

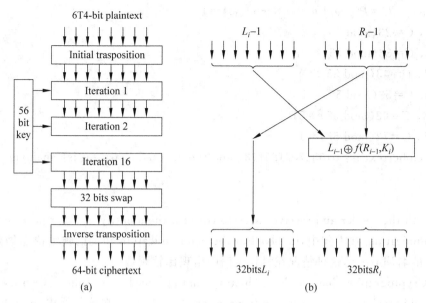

6T4-bit plaintext

Initial trasposition

56 bit key

Iteration 1

Iteration 2

Iteration 16

32 bits swap

Inverse transposition

64-bit ciphertext

(a)

L_i-1　　　R_i-1

$L_{i-1} \oplus f(R_{i-1}, K_i)$

32bitsL_i　　　32bitsR_i

(b)

Figure 7.4　The DES

IV. The public-key algorithm

Public-key cryptography requires each user to have two keys: a **public key** and a **private key**. The public key is used by the entire world for encrypting messages. Private keys are owned only by users who need for decrypting messages. **RSA** (Rivest, Shamir, Adleman) is an important public-key algorithm and much practical security is based on it.

The RSA method is based on some principles from number theory. The algorithm of RSA is as follows.

- Choose two large primes, p and q.
- Compute $n = p \times q$ and $z = (p-1) \times (q-1)$.
- Choose a number relatively prime to z and call it d.
- Find e such that $e \times d = 1 \bmod z$.

For example, to encrypt a message P, it is needed to compute $C = P^e (\bmod n)$. To decrypt C, $P = C^d (\bmod n)$ is computed. Therefore, the public key consists of the pair (e, n), and the private key consists of (d, n).

e.g. Using the RSA public key cryptosystem, with $a=1$, $b=2$, etc.. Using $p=5$, $q=11$, and $d=27$, find e and encrypt "abcdefg".

Analysis:

$n = p \times q = 5 \times 11 = 55$

$z = (p-1) \times (q-1) = 40$

$d = 27$

e such that $e \times d = 1 \bmod z$. $e = 3$

To encrypt a message P, compute $C = P^e (\bmod n)$.

So，$a=1$，$C=P^e(\bmod n)=1^3(\bmod 55)=1$

$b=2$，$C=2^3(\bmod 55)=8$

$c=3$，$C=3^3(\bmod 55)=27$

$d=4$，$C=4^3(\bmod 55)=9$

$e=5$，$C=5^3(\bmod 55)=15$

$f=6$，$C=6^3(\bmod 55)=51$

$g=7$，$C=7^3(\bmod 55)=13$

The ciphertext is：01082709155113，and the denoted character is：ahaioym.

Notes

① Both the sender and receiver need to confirm the identity of other party involved in the communication. 在本句中，involved in the communication 动词的被动语态做形容词修饰其前面的名词 party，这种情况在科技英语中出现比较频繁。

② Cryptography has a long history dating back to Julius Caesar, modern cryptographic techniques used in the Internet are based on it. 在这句话中，date back to 的意思是追溯到什么时候。

③ It focus on block ciphers, which take an n-bit block of plaintext as input and transform it using the key into n-bit block of cipher-text. 在科技英语中，定语从句出现的频率很高，句子有时比较深奥，在本句话中，which 引导定语从句，修饰其前面的 block ciphers。

New Words and Phrases

malicious	[məˈliʃəs]	adj.	怀恶意的;恶毒的
intentionally	[inˈtenʃənəli]	adv.	有意地;故意地
secrecy	[ˈsiːkrəsi]	n.	秘密;保密;隐蔽
authentication	[ɔːˌθentiˈkeiʃən]	n.	证明;鉴定
integrity	[inˈtegrəti]	n.	完整;完善;正直;诚实
confidentiality	[ˌkɔnfiˌdenʃiˈæləti]	n.	保密;机密
sensitive	[ˈsensitiv]	adj.	敏感的;感光的;易受伤害的
intruder	[inˈtruːdər]	n.	入侵者;干扰者;妨碍者
cryptography	[kripˈtɔgrəfi]	n.	密码术;密码系统
cipher	[ˈsaifə]	n.	密码;阿拉伯数字;零;暗号
code	[kəud]	n.	密码;法规;准则
disguise	[disˈgaiz]	vt.	掩饰;假装;假扮
encryption	[inˈkripʃn]	n.	加密
cryptanalyst	[kripˈtænəlist]	n.	密码破译者;密码专家
decryption	[diːˈkripʃn]	n.	译码(解释编码的数据)
inverse	[inˈvəːs]	adj.	倒转的;相反的
leftmost	[ˈleftməust]	adj.	最左边的

identical	[ai'dentikəl]	*adj.*	同一的；相同的

Computer Terminologies

substitution ciphers	替代密码
transposition ciphers	换位密码
Caesar cipher	恺撒密码
symmetric-key algorithm	对称密钥算法
public-key algorithm	公开密钥算法
Sniffer	嗅探器
cipher-text	密文
plaintext	明文
key	密钥
DES（Data Encryption Standard）	数据加密标准
public key	公钥
private key	私钥

RSA（Rivest，Shamir，Adleman）RSA 公钥加密算法是 1977 年由 Ron Rivest、Adi Shamirh 和 LenAdleman 在美国麻省理工学院开发的。RSA 取名来自三名开发者的名字。

Exercises

I. Translate the sentences into Chinese.

1. Network security problems can be divided roughly into three aspects：secrecy，authentication，message integrity.

2. Authentication deals with determining whom you are talking to before revealing **sensitive** information or entering into a business deal.

3. Cryptographic techniques allow a sender to disguise data so that an intruder can gain no information from the intercepted data.

4. We will use $C = E_K(P)$ to mean that the encryption of the plaintext P using key K gives the cipher-text C. Similarly，$P = D_K(C)$ represents the decryption of C to get the plaintext P.

5. The traditional encryption methods have been divided into two categories：substitution ciphers and transposition ciphers.

6. In a substitution cipher，each letter or group of letters is replaced by another letter or group of letters to disguise it.

7. DES（Data Encryption Standard）is one of symmetric-key algorithms and is widely adopted by the industry for use in security products.

8. Public-key cryptography requires each user to have two keys：a public key and a private key.

Extending Your Reading

Case of history—Code-breaking contests

First adopted by the US government in 1977, the Data Encryption Standard(DES) 56-bit algorithm is still widely used by financial services and other industries around the world to protect sensitive information. The company RSA Security has been sponsoring a series of DES-cracking contests to emphasize the need for encryption stronger than the current 56-bit standard. The challenge is to decrypt a message that has been encoded with 56-bit DES within a specified amount of time. Code breakers meet the challenge by exhaustively searching over all of the possible secret keys. RSA awards a \$10,000 prize to the winners.

The first DES Challenge, in 1997, was won by a team from Colorado that recovered the secret key in less than four months. Since then improved technology has made much faster exhaustive search efforts possible. In February 1998, Distributed. NET won RSA's DES Challenge Ⅱ-1 with a 41-day effort, and in July, the Electronic Frontier Foundation (EFF) won RSA's DES Challenge Ⅱ-2 when it cracked the DES message in 56 hours.

参考译文

网 络 安 全

不可计数的人使用网络来通信、购物、银行交易、在线办公,网络安全变得越来越重要。大多数的安全问题都是因为不怀好意的人有目的地想获得一些利益、得到注意或者伤害他人而产生的。图 7.1 列出了导致网络安全问题的一些人群。

攻击者	目 标
学生	喜欢窥探别人的电子邮件
破坏者	考验某人的安全系统;窃取数据
销售代表	声称代表整个欧洲,不仅仅是安道尔共和国
商人	想找到竞争对手的市场计划策略
离职雇员	被解雇之后实施报复
会计	挪用公司钱款
股票经纪人	否认自己通过电子邮件对顾客做过承诺
骗子	偷取信用卡号码再转让
间谍	了解敌人的军事或工业秘密
恐怖分子	偷取细菌战机密

图 7.1 引发起安全问题的人群和目标

网络安全问题可以大致分为三个方面:隐私、身份验证、信息完整性。隐私也叫做保密性,必须避免信息被未授权人的用户获取。身份验证确定在显示敏感信息或者在进入商业交易之前你正在跟谁交流。无论是发送者还是接收者都需要确定参与通信的另一方的身份。即使发送方和接收方能够彼此验证,也需要确定其通信的内容在通信中不会发生改变。也就是说,应该保持数据的完整性。

一个现实世界的网络入侵者能够监听和记录网络信息吗? 答案是肯定的。比如,包捕捉软件 Sniffer 用来被动接收通过设备网络接口的所有的帧。加密常常用来保证安全通信。

密码学

密码学有悠久的历史,可以追溯到 Julius Caesar,现代 Internet 中使用的密码学都基于它。加密技术允许发送方伪装数据,这样入侵者不能从窃取的数据获取信息。当然,接收方一定可以从伪装的数据中恢复原始数据。

图 7.2 显示了加密模型,包括一些重要的技术。密码是字节到字节或者位到位的转换,而不考虑信息的语言结构。加密是用另一个字或者符号来代替一个字。要加密的信息叫做明文。加密输出的结果叫做密文。明文通常通过一个带有密钥的函数转化为密文。我们使用 $C=E_K(P)$ 表示密文 C 是通过明文 P 使用密钥 K 加密获得。类似地,$P=D_K(C)$ 表示 P 是密文 C 解密获得。

传统的加密方法被分为两类:替代密码和换位密码。

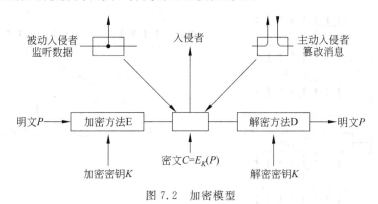

图 7.2　加密模型

替代密码

在替代加密中,每一个字母或者一组字母被另外一个字母或者一组字母代替伪装。恺撒密码是已知的最古老的密码。在这个方法中,字母 a 变成字母 D,b 变成 E,z 变成 C 等。比如,"apple"的恺撒密码就变成"DSSOH"。

换位密码

替代密码保持了明文字符的顺序而伪装了它们。相反,换位密码重组字母的顺序但是不伪装它们。明文垂直或者水平排列,如果需要填充矩阵。密文按列读出,从最小的关键字母开始。一个换位密码的例子如图 7.3 所示。

对称密钥算法

一般地,传统的加密算法很简单。现在,加密算法变得如此复杂以至于密码分析者即使获得了很多的加密文本也弄不清楚任何意思。有两种典型的加密算法:对称密钥算法、公钥算法。对称密钥算法使用同样的密钥来加密解密。它关注于分组密码,输入 n 位明文密

图 7.3　一个转置密码

码,使用密钥把它转换为 n 位密文块。加密算法既可以由硬件实现又可以由软件实现。

DES 是对称密钥中的一种,广泛用于工业界安全产品。工作过程如图 7.4 所示。明文按 64 位一起进行加密,产生 64 位密文。该算法有一个 56 位的密钥参数,有 19 个不同的阶段。第一个阶段是在 64 位明文上的独立于密钥的换位过程。最后一个阶段是这个换位过程的精确的逆过程。倒数第二个阶段是把最左边的 32 位与最右边的 32 位交换。剩下的 16 个阶段功能上相同,但是密钥带有不同的函数。算法指定可以和加密用同样的密钥解密。

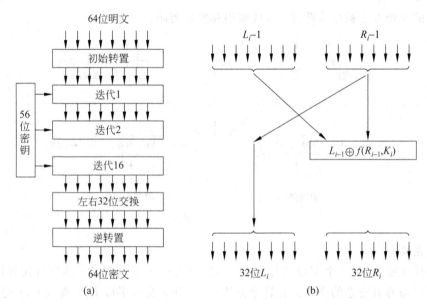

图 7.4　数据加密标准 DES

公开密钥算法

公开密钥加密算法要求每个用户有两个密钥:公钥和私钥。公钥被用于加密的全世界人拥有,私钥仅被那些需要解密的用户所有。RSA 是一个很重要的公钥算法,很多实际的安全策略都基于它。

RSA 算法是基于一些原则的数字理论。RSA 算法如下:

- 选择两个大素数,p 和 q。
- 计算 $n = p \times q$,且 $z = (p-1) \times (q-1)$。

- 选择一个与 z 互为素数的数，为 d。
- 找到一个 e 保证 $e \times d = 1 \bmod z$。

比如，加密一个信息 P，需要计算 $C = P^e (\bmod\ n)$。解密 C，需要计算 $P = C^d (\bmod\ n)$。因此，公钥包含了 (e, n)，私钥包含了 (d, n)。

比如，采用 RSA 公钥加密体系，$a = 1, b = 2$，等等。假如 $p = 5, q = 11, d = 27$；找出 e 然后加密"abcdefg"。

分析：

$n = p \times q = 5 \times 11 = 55$

$z = (p-1) \times (q-1) = 40$

$d = 27$

因为 $e \times d = 1 \bmod z$. 所以 $e = 3$。

加密信息 P，计算 $C = P^e (\bmod\ n)$。

因此，

$a = 1, C = P^e (\bmod\ n) = 1^3 (\bmod\ 55) = 1$

$b = 2, C = 2^3 (\bmod\ 55) = 8$

$c = 3, C = 3^3 (\bmod\ 55) = 27$

$d = 4, C = 4^3 (\bmod\ 55) = 9$

$e = 5, C = 5^3 (\bmod\ 55) = 15$

$f = 6, C = 6^3 (\bmod\ 55) = 51$

$g = 7, C = 7^3 (\bmod\ 55) = 13$

密文是：01082709155113，表示的字符是：ahaioym。

Unit 8　The New Network Technology

New Network Technologies

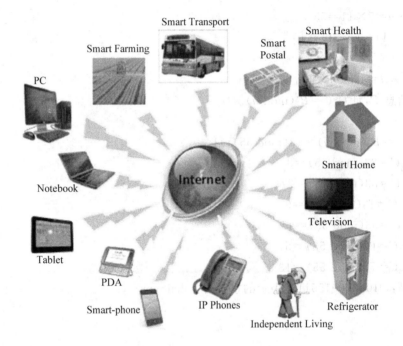

I. Introduction

With the development of network and communication technologies, many new technologies have emerged, such as **Internet of things (IoT)**, clouding computing and mobile networks.

II. Internet of Things

The concept of Internet of Things was proposed in 1999, which means all objects connecting to the Internet through information sensing devices such as the identification by **radio frequency (RFID)**, **wireless sensors**, **Global Positioning System (GPS)**, **Laser Scanner**, etc. [1] In IoT, everything has a unique identity which is different from each other and thus make a world network covers everything in the network. The model of IoT concept is shown in Figure 8.1.

The IoT have three basic characteristics. The first is the comprehensive perception which accesses information at anytime and anywhere by using the RFID, sensors and two-dimensional tags. The second is the reliable delivery which sends the real-time information

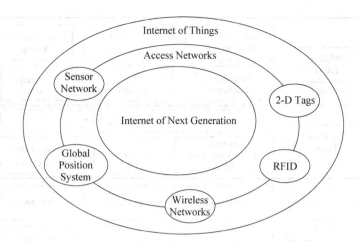

Figure 8.1   Model of IoT concept

accurately through the integration of telecommunications networks and the Internet. The third is the intelligent processing which uses cloud computing, **fuzzy recognition** and other intelligent computing technologies to analyze and process the massive data and information to control objects intelligently.

1. Architecture of the Internet of Things

Because of the above three basic characteristics of the IoT, the architecture of three-layer is generally approved, as shown in Figure 8.2. The sensor layer is used to sense data of objects; the network layer is used to transmit data information; the application layer is the top layer.

The sensor layer as the skin and the five sense **organs** of people is used to recognize objects and gather information by various types of sensing devices. They includes two-dimensional tags, RFID readers and tags, cameras, GPS, various sensors, video cameras and so on. Signals and information collect at these sensing devices are linked to the applications through the cloud computing platforms in the network layer.

The network layer is used to transmit and process information as the **"neural"** center and "brain" of the IoT. It includes the network integrated by communications and the Internet, network management center, information center and intelligent processing center, etc. The network layer transmits and processes information of the sensor layer and access layer.

The application layer achieves a wide range of intelligent applications by combining with the industry's needs. It is a deep incorporation of industries and the Internet.

2. Applications of the Internet of Things

The IoT can find its applications in almost every aspect of our daily life. Below are some of the examples.

(1) **Prediction** of natural disasters

The combination of sensors and their **autonomous** coordination and simulation will help to predict the occurrence of land-slides or other natural disasters and to take appropriate

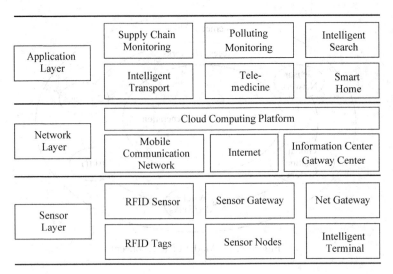

Figure 8.2　Three-layer Architecture of IoT

actions in advance.

(2) Industry applications

IoT can be applied in industry, such as **supply chain management**. Supply chain management is a process used by companies to ensure that their supply chain efficient and **cost-effective**. It can be aided by the IoT system. The idea of supply chain management is to manage a whole network of related businesses or partners involved in product manufacturing, delivery, services for customers.

(3) Design of smart building

The IoT has been suggested in construction of **smart building** in residential, commercial, industrial and government settings. A smart building can be a shopping mall or a home, a hospital or a **high-rise** office tower, which need monitoring and regulation of heating, lighting, environment changes and building security. Smart building technologies focus on bringing more detailed monitoring and sensing **"awareness"** to buildings.

(4) Medical application

The IoT can be applied in medical sector for saving lives or improving the quality of life. For example, monitoring health parameters, monitoring activities, support for independent living, monitoring medicines intake etc.

(5) Agriculture application

The applications of IoT in the agriculture include smart packaging of seeds, **fertilizer** and pest control mechanisms that respond to specific local conditions and indicate actions. Intelligent farming system will help agronomists to have better understanding of the plant growth models and to have efficient farming practices by having the knowledge of land conditions and climate variability. This will significantly increase the agricultural productivity by avoiding the inappropriate farming conditions.

3. Challenges of the Internet of Things

The IoT can change the shape of the Internet and can offer enormous economic

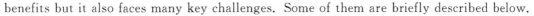

benefits but it also faces many key challenges. Some of them are briefly described below.

- Naming and Identity Management
- Interoperability and Standardization
- Information **Privacy**
- Data **confidentiality** and **encryption**
- Network security
- **Spectrum**

III. Cloud Computing

Cloud computing is a network-based environment that focuses on sharing computations or resources. Actually, clouds are Internet-based and it allows anyone connected to the Internet to use hardware and software on demand. In cloud environments, several kinds of virtual machines are hosted on the same physical server as infrastructure. Customers must only pay for what they use in the cloud and have not to pay for local resources such as storage or infrastructure.

Nowadays, there are three types of cloud environments: Public, Private, and **Hybrid clouds**. A public cloud is standard model which provides several resources, such as applications and storage, available to the public. Public cloud services may be free or not. Private Cloud refers to internal services of a business that is not available for ordinary people. Hybrid cloud is an environment that a company provides and controls some resources internally and has some others for public use. Also there is combination of private and public clouds that called Hybrid cloud. In this type, cloud provider has a service that has private cloud part which only accessible by **certified** staff and protected by firewalls from outside accessing and a public cloud environment which external users can access to it.

In the cloud environment, there are three major types of service: **SaaS** (Software as a Service), **PaaS** (Platform as a Service), and **IaaS** (Infrastructure as a Service), as shown in Figure 8.3. For having good and high performance, cloud provider must meet several management features to ensure improving RAS parameters of its service, such as:

- **Availability** management
- Access control management
- **Vulnerability** and problem management
- **Patch** and configuration management
- Countermeasure
- Cloud system using and access monitoring

Clouds are enabled by the progress in hardware, software, and networking technologies. These technologies play important roles in making cloud computing a reality. Most of these technologies are mature today to meet increasing demand. In the hardware area, the rapid progress in multi-core CPUs, memory chips, and disk arrays has made it possible to build faster data centers with huge amounts of storage space.[2]

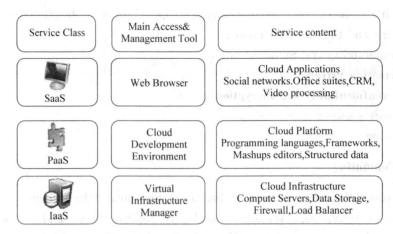

Figure 8.3 Cloud computing services

Resource **virtualization** enables rapid cloud **deployment** and disaster recovery. **Service-oriented** architecture also plays a vital role.

Notes

① The concept of Internet of Things was proposed in 1999, which means all objects connecting to the Internet through information sensing devices such as the identification by radio frequency (RFID), wireless sensors, Global Positioning System (GPS), Laser Scanner, etc. 在本句话中，which 引导的非限制性定语从句的主语是 The concept of Internet of Things。

② In the hardware area, the rapid progress in multi-core CPUs, memory chips, and disk arrays has made it possible to build faster data centers with huge amounts of storage space. 在本句话中，谓语 has，主语是 the rapid progress。

New Words and Phrases

organ	[ˈɔːgən]	n.	器官
neural	[ˈnjuərəl]	adj.	神经的
prediction	[priˈdikʃn]	n.	预言；预报
autonomous	[ɔːˈtɔnəməs]	adj.	自治的
cost-effective		adj.	有成本效益的；划算的
high-rise		adj.	超高层的；高楼的；高手把的
awareness	[əˈweənəs]	n.	认识；觉察；意识
fertilizer	[ˈfəːtilaizə]	n.	肥料
privacy	[ˈprivəsi]	n.	隐居；隐私；秘密
confidentiality	[ˌkɔnfiˌdenʃiˈæləti]	n.	保密；机密
encryption	[inˈkripʃn]	n.	加密
spectrum	[ˈspektrəm]	n.	系列；范围；光谱；[科]频谱
certify	[ˈsəːtifai]	vt.	证明；保证；证实；颁发证书

availability	[əˌveiləˈbiləti]	n.	有效；有用；有益；可用性
vulnerability	[ˌvʌlnərəˈbiləti]	n.	易受攻击；脆弱；[计]漏洞
patch	[pætʃ]	n.	小片；补丁；眼罩
virtualization	[vɜːtʃʊəlaiˈzeiʃn]	n.	虚拟化
deployment	[diˈplɔimənt]	n.	部署；展开

Computer Terminologies

Internet of things (IoT)	物联网
radio frequency identification (RFID)	无线射频识别
wireless sensors	无线传感器
Global Positioning System (GPS)	全球定位系统
Laser Scanner	激光扫描仪
fuzzy recognition	模糊识别
supply chain management	供应链管理
smart building	智能大厦
Hybrid clouds	混合云
SaaS	软件即服务
PaaS	平台即服务
IaaS	架构即服务
Service-oriented	面向服务

Exercises

Answer the questions.

1. What is IoT?
2. What are the characteristics of IoT?
3. Describe the architecture of IoT.
4. What is cloud computing?
5. Describe the types of cloud computing.

Extending Your Reading

An interview with Steve Jobs

Apple is famous for its entertaining, world-class product presentations, that attract press coverage (read: free advertising) from the entire world—and there is no debate as to who built this reputation. Steve Jobs's celebrity and charisma made him "the closest thing to a rock star in the world of business". During his second tenure at Apple, between 1997 and 2011, he appeared 4 to 7 times a year (when he was healthy, of course) to unveil new products during one of his trademark 'keynotes'. While he was notoriously a capricious speaker who refused to rehearse in his late twenties, he perfected his art at NeXT, and came back to Apple as the best showman of the industry.

参考译文

网络新技术

随着网络和通信技术的发展,许多的新技术涌现出来,如物联网、云计算、移动网络。

物联网

物联网的概念是在 1999 年提出来的,这意味着所有的物体通过信息感应设备接入Internet,这些设备有无线射频识别、无线传感器、全球定位系统、激光扫描仪,等等。在物联网中,一切都有一个彼此不相同的唯一标志,因此使世界构成了一个覆盖一切的网络。物联网概念模型如图 8.1 所示。

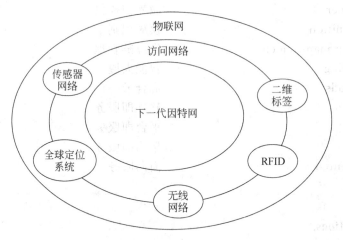

图 8.1　物联网概念模型

物联网有三个基本的特点。第一个特点是全面感知,它通过无线射频、感应器和二维标志在任何时刻任何地点接入信息。第二个特点是可信传输,它通过电信网络和 Internet 的整合准确地发送实时信息。第三个特点是智能处理,它使用云计算、模糊认知以及其他的智能技术去分析和处理大数据和信息来智能地控制对象。

物联网的体系结构

由于物联网的上述三个特点,三层体系结构得到认同,如图 8.2 所示。感知层用来感知物体的数据;网络层用来传输数据信息;应用层位于顶层。

感知层如人的皮肤和人的五个器官用来认识物体,以及通过各种类型的感知设备收集信息。它们包含二维标签、无线射频识别阅读器和标签、摄像机、全球定位系统、多样的感应器、视频摄像机等。在这些设备收集的信号和信息通过网络层的云计算平台连接到应用。

网络层是物联网的大脑和神经中心用于传输和处理信息。它包括集成通信的网络、Internet、网络管理中心、信息中心和智能处理中心等。网络层传输和处理感知层和接收层的信息。

应用层通过结合工业的需求实现广泛的智能应用。它是工业和 Internet 的深度组合。

物联网的应用

在日常生活中的各个方面都能找到物联网的应用。以下就是一些例子。

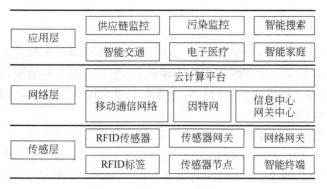

图 8.2　物联网的三层结构

（1）自然灾害的预测

传感器及其自主协调和仿真的结合将有助于预测滑坡或其他的自然灾害的发生，并提前采取适当的策略。

（2）工业应用

物联网能够被应用在工业中，如提供供应链管理。供应链管理是一个由公司保证其供应链有效和成本有效的过程。它可由物联网系统辅助实现。供应链管理的思想是：管理涉及产品制造、传输、客户服务的相关商家或合作伙伴的整个网络。

（3）智慧建筑设计

物联网被提出构造住宅的、商业的、工业的以及政府的智慧建筑。智能建筑可以是一个购物中心或者一个家庭住宅、一个医院或一栋高耸的办公楼，它们需要监控、有调节的加热、照明、环境变化以及构建安全。智能建筑技术专注于更详细的检测和可感知"意识"的建筑。

（4）医疗应用

物联网可以应用于医疗部门挽救生命或者改进生活质量。例如，监视健康参数、监视活动、支持独立生活、监控服用药物等。

（5）农业应用

物联网在农业中的应用包括种子的智能包装、施肥以及虫害的控制机制应对当地的具体条件和指示行动。智能农业系统帮助农业专家更好地理解植物生长模型以及通过了解土地条件和气候变化并采取有效的农场措施。避免不合适的农场条件将极大地提高农业生产率。

物联网的挑战

物联网可以改变 Internet 的形态，提供巨大的经济效益但是它也面临很多挑战。其中一些简短描述如下。

- 命名和身份管理
- 互操作性和标准化
- 信息隐私权
- 数据保密和加密
- 网络安全
- 频谱

云计算

云计算是基于网络环境,它关注于共享计算能力或资源。实际上,云是基于 Internet 的,它允许任何人根据需求使用硬件和软件接入 Internet。在云环境中,几种虚拟机作为基础设施位于同一个物理服务器。客户只需为他在云里使用的东西付费,不需要为本地资源如存储和基础设施付费。

如今,有三种类型的云环境:公共云环境、私有云环境以及混合云。公共云是标准模型,它给公众提供了几种可用的资源,如应用、存储。公共云服务可能是免费的也可能不是。私有云指的是商业内部服务,它不面向普通人。混合云是一个环境,它由一个公司提供,控制了一些内部资源,有一些资源为公共使用。也有私有云和公共云的结合叫做混合云。这种类型中,云提供者有一种服务具有私有云部分只能由认证员工才可以访问,由防火墙保护防止从外面接入,对于公共云环境来说,外部的用户可以接入。

在云环境中,主要有三种类型服务:SaaS(软件即为服务)、PaaS(平台即为服务)和 IaaS(设施即为服务),如图 8.3 所示。要有好的高的性能,云提供者必须满足几个管理性质来保证改进服务的 RAS 参数,如:

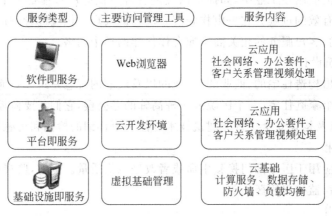

图 8.3　云计算服务

- 可用性管理。
- 接入控制管理。
- 漏洞和问题管理。
- 包和配置管理。
- 对策。
- 云系统使用和接入监控。

云是硬件、软件和网络技术进步的结果。这些技术在云计算变成现实方面起了很大的作用。现今这些技术的大部分已成熟能满足日益增加的需求。在硬件领域,多核 CPU、内存芯片、磁盘阵列的快速发展已经使得构建更快的大容量数据中心成为可能。资源虚拟化支持快速云发布和灾难恢复。面向服务的体系架构也起到了重要的作用。

Unit 9　Translation Skills of Computer Network English

计算机网络英语翻译技巧

一、计算机网络英语特点

计算机网络英语与普通英语有很大的区别,主要在于其内容具有很强的专业性,以表达科技概念、理论、事实为主要目的。与普通英语相比,它更注重客观事实和真理,要求逻辑性强,条理规范,表达准确、精练、正式。它有如下特点:

- 长句多。
- 被动语态使用频繁。
- 虚拟语气表达假设或者建议。
- 广泛使用祈使句。
- 名词性词组多。
- 非限定动词使用频率高。
- 介词短语多。
- 常用 It…句型结构。
- 单个动词比动词词组使用频繁。
- 常使用动词或者名词演化成的形容词。
- 专业术语多。
- 缩略词、缩略语经常出现。
- 半技术词汇多。
- 公式、表格、插图使用比较多。

二、计算机网络英语翻译原则

翻译是用一种语言形式把另一种语言形式的内容重新表达出来的语言实践活动。它要求既要忠实于原作,又要力求规范。

翻译既要使译文忠实于原文,又要通顺可读,所以就不能局限于逐词对译,必须采用适当的词性转换,句子成分转换,甚至句型转换。科技英语中名词化结构使用较多,而汉语中动词用得较多,英译汉时名词转换成动词就是常见的现象之一。另外,汉语中没有冠词、关系代词、关系副词、分词、不定式、动名词等。翻译上述词类时要进行转换处理。

无论是将英语翻译成汉语,还是将汉语翻译成英语,最重要的是要理解两套语言体系的相同点以及不同点。而造成翻译的难点归根结底在于语言差异和文化差异。因此要做到精准翻译,必须了解两大语言体系的差异。英语和汉语两大语言体系的差异主要体现在英语有形态的变化,汉语没有严格意义形态的变化,英语词序比较灵活,汉语词序比较固定。英语中还经常使用连词、冠词、不定冠词。

此外,翻译时应做到深刻理解原文内容,理解原文句子之间的结构、主从关系,辨别清楚主语、谓语、宾语、表语、状语等句子成分,在翻译时做到正确地选择词义,有时需要转换表达或者引申表达,有时需要增减词语,有时需要改变词序,有时需要词性转换以及句子成分的转换。通读全文,不要遇到生词就停下来查字典,影响思维。根据原文上下文做出正确的理解、选择和变换。

语言的表达形式是多样的、灵活的,翻译时只要把握了"忠实于原作、力求规范"的原则,译文可以有多种形式,它不是套用固定公式,一成不变的。本章列出了一些翻译时值得借鉴的技巧,以便帮助读者更好地掌握计算机英语翻译。

三、计算机网络英语词汇的构成特点

计算机网络专业英语中除了常出现的名词、动词、形容词、冠词等普通词汇之外,其特点为常出现以下的 3 类词汇。

1. 技术词汇

这类词的意义狭窄,一般只用在各自的专业领域中,这类词一般较长并且越长词义越狭窄,出现的频率也不高。

例如,multicasting(组播)、unicasting(单播)、synchronization(同步)、electromagnetic(电磁的)、decibels(分贝)、half duplex(半双工)、full duplex(全双工)等。

2. 次技术词汇

次技术词汇是指不受上下文限制,在各个专业中出现频率都很高的词,在不同的专业领域表现为不同的意义。

例如,architecture 在计算机英语中表示为"体系结构、架构",在建筑行业中表示为"建筑学、建筑风格";virus 在医学中为"病毒",在计算机中也为"病毒",都是指有害的东西,但不是同一种,等等。

3. 功能词

功能词包括介词、连词、冠词、代词等,主要起到句子结构的作用。尤其是连词、冠词和代词,没有特定的意义,但确是句子不可缺少的成分。研究表明,在英语中出现频率最高前十位词是功能词,其顺序为: the、of、in、and、to、is、that、for、are、be。

例如,Along with the good comes the bad. 祸福相依。本句总共 7 个词,定冠词 the 在本句中出现两次,介词 with 出现一次。

四、计算机网络英语构词法

随着计算机的出现,相应的新生的英语词汇出现了,在计算机网络英语中,有的词汇借用公共英语中的词汇,有的借用外来语言词汇,如希腊语、拉丁语,有的是人为构造的词汇。除此之外,计算机网络英语主要可分为以下几类词汇。

1. 合成词

合成词在计算机网络英语中占了非常大的一部分,翻译时直接由组成的词意组合翻译,有时需稍做变换。其合成形式多样,有名词＋动词、形容词＋名词、动词＋副词、名词＋动词、介词＋名词、形容词＋动词等。其表现形式多数以"-"连接单词构成。如：

ill-formed 不规范的　　　　　　　general-purpose 通用的

packet-switched 分组交换　　　　omni-directional 全方位的

store-and-forward 存储转发　　　end-to-end 端到端

round-trip 双程旅行　　　　　　　multi-inputs 多输入

long-term 长期的　　　　　　　　newly-booted 新启动地

cost-effective 有成本效益的　　　fixed-format 固定格式的

object-oriented 面向对象　　　　platform-independent 跨平台

public-source 公开源代码　　　　component-based 基于组件

cipher-text 密文　　　　　　　　symmetric-key 对称密钥

public-key 公开密钥　　　　　　Service-oriented 面向服务

high-rise 高楼的　　　　　　　　would-be 自称的

base-band 基带　　　　　　　　electronic-commerce 电子商务

variable-sized 变长的　　　　　long-term 长期的,长远

real-time 实时的

随着词汇的频繁使用,合成词中的连接符被省略掉形成一个独立的单词。如：

over＋lap＝overlap　　　　　　check＋sum＝checksum

times＋tamp＝timestamp　　　code＋word＝codeword

pay＋load＝payload　　　　　time＋out＝timeout

net＋work＝network　　　　　loop＋back＝loopback

frame＋work＝framework　　gate＋way＝gateway

over＋head＝overhead

2. 派生词

这类词汇是通过派生法构成的,在计算机网络英语中占了大部分,它是根据已经有的词,加上前缀或者后缀来构成新词。前缀和后缀有各种形式。

常用前缀：

a 定,无,离开,往外,到,向,在,在内,在上　　如 asymmetric

co 共同,完全,相互　　　　　如 coefficient

de 下,减少,降低,否定　　　　如 decrement decryption

dis 不,未,否定,相反　　　　　如 discard Disconnection disguise

electro 电子的　　　　　　　如 electromagnetic

ex 出,出自,向外　　　　　　如 exchange

en 使,在内,往里不　　　　　如 encryption

geo 地理的　　　　　　　　　如 geographical

hex 十六进制的	如 hexadecimal
In 不,非,入,内心	如 inherit infrared incoming interval
metro 大	如 metropolitan
micro 微,微小	如 microwave
mis 错误,坏	如 misleading
multi 多,多的	如 multicasting multiplexing multiparty multithread
on 在……之上	如 online
poly 多,复	如 polynomial polymorphism
pre 预先,在前	如 Prediction
re 再,重复	如 retransmission
super 超级,过分	如 supercomputer
sub 子,次	如 substantial subnet subtask Subnetting submask
tel 远,电	如 telecommunication contention
un 反,不,非	如 Unnumbered unambiguously unregulate
up 在……上,升级	如 Upgrade
under 在……之下,不足	如 underlying
常用后缀:	
ble 能……的,可……的,易于……的	如 accessible variable
cious ……的	如 malicious
er ……者,……人,……物	如 Repeater remainder Router resolver intruder fertilizer Laser
ment 行为,状态,过程	如 deployment agreement
or ……的人,……的物	如 conductor vector
tion 行为的过程,结果,状况	如 amplification telecommunication notation simulation encapsulation authentication
sion 行为,状态,过程	如 division collision
ty 性质,状态,抽象情况	如 confidentiality Availability Vulnerability
tive ……的	如 sensitive

五、计算机网络英语中的缩略词

缩略词是将较长的单词取其首部或主干构成与原词同义的短单词,或者将一组短语的各个单词首字母拼接为一个大写的首字母串。缩略词在计算机中频繁使用。

以下列出了本书中出现的部分缩略词:

TCP/IP(Transmission Control Protocol/Internet Protocol)	传输控制/网络通信协议
ISP(Internet Service Provider)	网络服务提供者
LAN(local area network)	局域网
MAN(Metropolitan Area Network)	城域网
HTTP(hyper text transfer protocol)	超文本传输协议

TDM(Time Division Multiplexing)   时分复用
CRC(Cyclic Redundancy Check)   循环冗余校验码

六、计算机网络英语中的专业术语

在计算机领域中出现了很多只用于本领域的专业词汇或者短语,叫做计算机术语。以下列出了本书中出现的部分计算机术语:

computer networ 计算机网络   packet-switched 分组交换
broadband 宽带   WiFi(Wireless Fidelity)无线保真
Mobile Internet 移动互连网   World Wide Web 万维网
Internet 因特网   TCP/IP 传输控制/网络通信协议
IMP 接口信息处理器   subnet 子网
host 主机   backbone 主干网
supercomputer 巨型机   regional network 区域网
ISP 网络服务提供者   TCP/IP reference modelTCP/IP 参考模型
TCP/IP protocol stackTCP/IP 协议栈   presentation layer 表示层

专业术语在翻译时一般采用"意译"法,如 three-way handshake(三次握手)、slow start(慢开始)、congestion avoidance(拥塞避免),有少部分无法意译可以采用"音译",如 bit(比特)、decibels(分贝,音量的单位),还有极少部分需要"形译",如 I-shaped(工字形)、Y-connection(Y 形连接)。

七、计算机网络英语中常用语法

1. 动词不定式

非谓语动词中的一种,不能做谓语,表示为 to do sth,它能做主语、表语、宾语、定语、宾语补足语,可以有自己的宾语、状语以及宾语补足语;还有时态和语态的变化。

1)做主语

例如:

Given any two codewords,10001001 and 10110001,it is possible to determine how many corresponding bits differ. 真正的主语是动词不定式短语,it 只是形式主语。

译文:给出任两个码字 10001001 和 10110001,能够确定有多少相应的位数不同。

2)做宾语

例如:

Various glasses and plastics can be used to make optical fibers. 动词不定式做宾语。

译文:各种各样的玻璃和塑料用于制作光纤。

3)做表语

例如:

The main task of the data link layer is to provide for the reliable transfer of information across the physical link,including sending frames with the necessary synchronization,error control and flow control. 动词不定式放在系动词后面做表语。

译文：数据链路层的主要任务是提供信息通过物理链路的可靠传输，包括必要的数据同步、错误控制以及流控制。

4）做状语

例如：

To achieve its goals, the network layer must know about the topology of the communication subnet and choose appropriate paths through it with load balancing. 动词不定式做状语，表示目的、程度、结果、范围、原因等。

译文：为了达到目的，网络层必须知道关于通信子网的拓扑，选择合适的路径通过并保持负载平衡。

5）做宾语补足语

例如：

NSF（the U. S. National Science Foundation）funded some regional networks that connected to the backbone to allow users at thousands of universities, research labs, libraries, and museums to access any of the supercomputers and to communicate with one another. 在本句中，动词不定式做宾语的补足语。Backbone 是 connected to 的宾语，to allow 做它的宾语补足语，to access 和 to communicate 做 users 的补足语。

译文：NSF 资助了一些连接到主干网的区域网，它允许成千上万的大学、研究所、图书馆、博物馆的用户接入任何一台超级计算机，彼此相互交流。

6）动词不定式的被动语态

例如：

It manages the abstract data structures and allows higher-level data structures to be defined and exchanged. 动词不定式做了宾语补足语，且表示为被动语态。

译文：会话层管理抽象的数据结构，并允许高层数据结构被定义和交换。

7）做定语

例如：

There are a variety of ways to get frames from one cable to another. 动词不定式做定语修饰前面的名词 ways。

译文：有各种各样的方法获得从一根线缆发往另一根线缆的帧。

2. 分词

分词也是非谓语动词中的一种，不能做谓语，它分过去分词和现在分词。规则动词的现在分词表现为 do＋ing 形式，过去分词表现为 do＋ed 构成；不规则动词分词形式构成不规则。在句子中具有形容词词性、副词词性，可做句子的定语、表语、状语和补足语。

现在分词

1）做定语

例如：

Just as you get comfortable with your campus-wide network, mobile Internet using wireless connection appeared that can be used by anyone at anytime and anywhere. 做主语 mobile Internet 的定语，修饰说明主语的情况。

译文：

当你还在悠然自在地使用校园网时，让人在任何时候、任何地点都能使用无线接入的移动互联网出现了。

The computer network is such a network consisting of two or more computers that are linked in order to share resources, exchange files, or allow electronic communications.

2）做主语补足语

例如：

The complete network, including the backbone and the regional networks, was called NSFNET. 现在分词短语，修饰主语 the complete network，补充说明主语的组成。

译文：完整的网络，包括主干网和区域网，叫做 NSFNET。

The resource subnet is composed of all hosts connected to the Internet, and the communication subnet consists of a large number of networks and routers connecting such networks.

3）做状语

例如：

It is worth devoting some time to point out applications of computer networks. 现在分词做状语，实际也是一种固定搭配，be worth doing sth。

译文：值得花时间列出计算机网络的应用。

4）做主语补足语

例如：

Using this technology, employees at distant locations can hold a meeting, seeing and hearing each other and even writing on a shared virtual blackboard. 补充说明主语 employees，详细描述开会的状态。

译文：使用这种视频技术，相距甚远的员工可以召开会议，能相互看见、听见甚至还能在一块共享的虚拟黑板上写字。

The resource subnet is composed of all hosts connected to the Internet, and the communication subnet consists of a large number of networks and routers connecting such networks.

过去分词

1）做定语

例 1：

With the increasing of the number of the networks, machines and users connected to the ARPANET grew rapidly and TCP/IP gradually became the only official protocol and Internet was born in 1983 in result. 做定语修饰 machines 和 users，表示连接入 ARPANET 的机器和用户。

译文：随着计算机网络、接入 ARPANET 的机器以及用户数量的快速增加，TCP/IP 逐渐变成了唯一的官方协议，Internet 最终于 1983 年产生了。

例 2：

Since having a wired connection is impossible in cars and airplanes, there is a lot of interest in wireless networks. 过去分词做定语，修饰 connection。

译文：既然在汽车和飞机内，有线连接是不可能的，那么无线网络的发展则有很多益处。

例3：

Using this technology, employees at distant locations can hold a meeting, seeing and hearing each other and even writing on a shared virtual blackboard. 做定语修饰 virtual blackboard，表示共享的。

译文：使用这种视频技术，相距甚远的员工可以召开会议，能相互看见、听见甚至还能在一块共享的虚拟黑板上写字。

2）做状语

例如：

The feature of the second stage is the three-level architecture used in the Internet. 做状语修饰 architecture。

译文：第二阶段的特点是用于 Internet 的三层体系结构。

3）做补足语

例如：

Local area networks, generally called LANs, are privately-owned networks within a single building or campus of up to a few kilometers in size. 做补足语，补充说明主语 Local area networks。

译文：局域网，一般简称为 LAN，指的是一栋建筑内或者几千米范围内的校园私有网络。

3. 动名词

动名词的形式和现在分词的形式具有相同的结构，但是其用法和意义不同，动名词具有名词的词性，在句子中主要充当主语、宾语、定语、表语。

做定语

例如

Sharing resource and data communication are the main function of computer networks. 现在分词短语做定语，修饰资源。

译文：资源共享和数据通信是计算机网络中的主要功能。

4. 被动语态

被动语态在计算机网络英语中广泛使用，因为被动语态比主动语态更能客观描述事情。通常强调动作的承受者时，经常采用被动语态；当动作的执行者是物时也常用被动语态；当大家已经清楚动作的执行者而没有必要说出来时，可以用被动语态；当不想说出或者不知道动作的执行者时，可以使用被动语态。不同时态的被动语态形式不同。

其表现形式为：

主语＋be＋(vt)过去分词

Local area networks, generally called LANs, are privately-owned networks within a single building or campus of up to a few kilometers in size. 强调动作的承受者 LAN。

译文：局域网，一般简称为 LAN，指的是一栋建筑内或者几千米范围内的校园私有网络。

被动语态翻译时通常通过"把"、"被"来体现，被动语态翻译时，一般采取以下方法：

（1）翻译成汉语的主动句。

① 英文原文中的主语在译文中做主语，往往在译文中使用"加以"、"经过"、"用来"等词体现原文的被动语态。

例如：

The computers on a network may be linked through cables, telephone lines, radio waves, satellites and so on. 在此句中，动作的执行者是物。

译文：网络上的计算机可以通过有线、电话线、无线电波、卫星等连接起来。

② 将英语原文中的主语翻译为宾语，同时增加泛指性的词语（人们、大家）做主语。

例如：

At the same time, the connection of two or more networks is called an internetwork. 省略了主语，动作的执行者为大家所熟知的。

译文：与此同时，我们把两个或者多个网络的连接叫做网络互连。

③ 将英文原文中的 by、in、for 等做状语的介词短语经常翻译成"由于"、"由"、"经过"、"通过"、"因为"等。

例如：

It is decremented by one by each router that forwards the packet. If the value of hop limit reaches zero, the packet is discarded.

译文：它由转发它的每一个路由器减 1。如果此字段的值变为 0，那么丢弃此分组。

④ 翻译成汉语的无主句。

例如：

Since many addresses will have many zeros inside them, three optimizations have been authorized.

译文：由于很多地址包含了很多 0 在里面，提出三种优化方法可以使用。

（2）翻译成汉语的被动句。常用"被"、"给"、"遭"、"挨"、"为……所"、"使"、"由"、"受到"、"得到"等表示。

A lot of these problems could be solved if the technology of the computer security is well established. 前面一句不清楚动作的执行者，"谁去解决问题？"所以采用被动语态，后一句的动作执行者仍然不清楚，所以采用被动语态。

译文：如果计算机安全技术很好地确立，许多的问题可以得到解决。

5. 定语从句

定语从句，顾名思义，在句子中起定语作用，修饰一个名词或代词。被定语从句修饰的词叫做先行词，定语从句通常位于其后。定语从句通常由关系代词 that、which、who、whom、whose 以及关系副词 when、where、why、how 引导。关系代词和关系副词往往放在先行词和从句之间，起联系作用。同时还担任一定的语法成分如主语、宾语、定语和状语等。

The network layer controls the operation of the subnet and is the lowest layer that deals with end-to-end transmission. 在本句中，that 指代网络层。

译文：网络层控制子网的操作，它是处理端到端传输的最低一层。

定语从句分为：限制性定语从句和非限制性定语从句。它们在计算机英语中出现非常频繁，而且可以使得句型结构非常复杂。

限制性定语从句

限制性定语从句与先行词关系密切。主句和从句之间不用逗号隔开。一般先译定语从句，再译先行词。如果定语从句修饰人，在句子中做主语，一般用关系代词 who，也可用 that，且不能省略；若为宾语则先行词应用 whom，经常可以省略。表示所属则用 whose。

限制性定语从句修饰物则用 that 较多，也可以用 which。在句中可以做主语、宾语；若为宾语，大多数情况可省略。

Furthermore, all this must be done efficiently and in a way that isolates the upper layers from the inevitable changes in the hardware technology. 在句子中做主语。

译文：再者，所有的这些都必须高效完成，在一定程度上把高一层和硬件技术上不可避免的变化隔绝开。

An analog signal is one in which the signal intensity varies in a smooth fashion over time. 在句子中做介词的宾语。

译文：模拟信号是一种强度随着时间平滑改变的信号。

In any broadcast network, the key issue is how to determine who gets to use the channel when there is competition for it, and the corresponding protocols belong to multiple access protocols. 在本句中，关系代词做主语。

译文：在任何的广播网络中，最关键的问题是当竞争产生时，如何决定谁使用信道，而相应使用的协议则属于多点接入协议。

非限制性定语从句

非限制性定语从句与先行词关系比较松散，常用逗号隔开，翻译成汉语时从句常单独翻译成一句。非限制性定语从句即使被删除也不会影响主句的意思。非限制性定语从句在修饰人时，先行词用 who、whom、whose；修饰物时用 which；修饰地点时用 where；修饰时间用 when 来引导。

LANs can be connected by bridges or switches, which operate in the data link layer.

译文：局域网由网桥或交换机连接，这些设备工作在数据链路层。

In order to illustrate how the algorithm works, we take an undirected and weighted graph of Figure 4.1 as an example, where the weights represent distance.

译文：为了表明算法如何工作，我们以图 4.1 中无向带权图为例，在图中，权表示距离。

6. 状语从句

状语从句在句子中起副词的作用，做状语；修饰主句中的动词、形容词等。可表示时间、原因、目的、结果、条件、比较、方式、让步、地点等不同含义。翻译时，分清主句和从句之间的逻辑关系，根据目的语言的习惯选择翻译主句在前还是从句在前。

时间状语从句：常用来引导时间状语从句的从属连词有

When 当……的时候

whenever 每当

after 在……之后

before 在……之前

as 当……;一边……一边

as soon as 一……就

while 在期间

till/until 直到

since 自从

once 曾经(等等)。

地点状语从句：常用的连接词有

Where 在……地方;那里

wherever 无论哪里(等等)。

原因状语从句：常用的连接词有

Because 因为……

since 既然

as 由于

now that 即使(等等)。

条件状语从句：引起条件状语从句的连词有

If 如果

unless 除非

once 一旦

as/so long as 只要(等等)。

目的状语从句：引起目的状语从句的连词有

so that 以便

in order that 以便(等等)。

结果状语从句：引起结果状语从句的连词有

So that 结果是;以至

so/such…that 如此……以至于(等等)。

让步状语从句：引起让步状语从句的连词有

Though 虽然

although 虽然

as 尽管

even if/even though 即使

no matter who/what/how 无论谁/无论什么/无论怎样

whoever 不管是谁

however 无论怎样(等等)。

方式状语从句：引起方式状语从句的词语一般有

As 正如;按照

as if/ as though 好像。

比较状语从句：引起比较状语从句的词语一般有

As…as 和……一样

not as/so…as 与……不一样

than 比。

例如：

Since many addresses will have many zeros inside them，three optimizations have been authorized. 表示原因的状语从句。

译文：由于许多地址中包含很多 0 在里面,三个优化方法被授权。

You can't use *structures*，*unions*，or *typedefs* because they have gone. 表示原因的状语从句。

译文：不可以使用 structure、union、typedef,因为它们已经消失了。

If people need to be on-line all the time，it is the most appropriate choice for mobile users to use wireless transmission. 表示条件的状语从句。

译文：如果需要一直在线,那么移动用户最合适的选择是使用无线传输。

7. 英汉物称与人称的比较

英语常用物称表达法,即不用人称来叙述,而让事物以客观的口气呈现出来。

汉语则较注重主体思维,往往从自我出发来叙述客观事物,或倾向于描述人及其行为或状态,因而常用人称。汉语重人称,英语重物称,这一特点主要表现在如何使用主语和动词这两方面。

英语可用人称主语表达,也常用非人称主语表达。用非人称主语表达时,往往注重什么事发生在什么人身上,而汉语则较常用人称主语表达,往往注重什么人怎样了。

如下几则例子：

英语：What happened to you?

中文：你发生什么了？

英语：What does it actually mean to be on the Internet?

中文：在线到底是指什么意思呢？

英语：It is worth devoting some time to point out applications of computer networks.

中文：值得我们花一些时间来指出计算机网络的应用。

英语用非人称主语的句子大体可以分为以下两大类：

(1) 用抽象名词或无生命的事物名称作主语,同时经常使用本来表示人的动作或行为的动词作其谓语。

例如：

It offers various services，including dialog control，token management，and synchronization. 在本句中 it 用来代替 session layer。

译文：会话层提供各种各样的服务,包括对话控制、令牌管理、同步。

It defines an official packet format and protocol called IP (Internet Protocol). 本句中用来指代无生命事物网络层。

译文：它定义了官方数据包格式和 IP 协议。

（2）用非人称代词"it"做主语。"it"除了用来代替除人以外的生物或事物之外，还广泛用作填补词。

例如：

The Internet makes it possible to find information quickly，but a lot of it is ill-informed，misleading，or downright wrong. 在本句中第一个 it 用做填补词，第二个 it 用来代表信息。

译文：Internet 使得可以快速找到信息，但是很多信息是不规范的、误导的或者甚至完全错误的。

It is clear that there must be a high degree of cooperation between two computer networks. 在本句中 it 做填补词。

译文：很清楚的是两台机器之间必须高度合作。

附录 部分习题答案

Unit 2

Section A

Ⅰ. 1. 2000bps   2. 30dB   3. Yes, I can. It is 20Mbps.

Ⅱ. c, d, a, b

Section B

Ⅰ. unguided, twisted pair, copper, radiates, telephone system, amplification, repeaters, analog, unshielded, coaxial cable, An optical fiber, multimode fiber, single-mode fiber, wireless, Radio, pass through, Infrared, artificial, telecommunications

Section C

Ⅰ. 1. circuit switching, packet switching   2. store-and-forward

3. telephone network   4. communication subnet   5. transmitted

Unit3

Section A

Ⅰ. 1. No. Hamming codes can only correct single errors.

2. 10, 21   3. 11010110111110

Ⅱ. 1. Hamming code, CRC   2. redundant   3. codeword   4. odd

5. Modulo 2 arithmetic   6. division   7. checksum

Section C

Ⅱ. 1. senses, idle, collision, abruptly, binary exponential back-off algorithm

2. notation, segments, base-band

Section D

Ⅱ. 1. hub   2. flooding algorithm, backward learning   3. transparent

4. cut-through switches, store-and-forward switches   5. interconnecting

6. forward

Unit 6

Section B

Ⅱ. 1. simulation   2. XML   3. simulator   4. plotting

5. object-oriented, inheritance   6. multithreading   7. component-based

参 考 文 献

[1] (美)Behrouz A. Forouzan, Firouz Mosharraf. Computer Networks：A Top-Down Approach[M]. 北京：机械工业出版社,2012

[2] Kurose J F, Ross K W, 陈鸣. 计算机网络：自顶向下方法[J]. 北京：机械工业出版社,2009

[3] 谢希仁. 计算机网络(第 5 版)[M]. 北京：电子工业出版社,2008

[4] Andrew S. Tanenbaum. 计算机网络(第 5 版)[M]. 严伟,潘爱民译. 北京：清华大学出版社,2012

[5] Andrew S. Tanenbaum. Computer Networks. 5th Edition. [M]. 北京：机械工业出版社,2011

[6] 施晓秋. 计算机网络实训[M]. 北京：高等教育出版社,2008

[7] 方路平,刘世华,陈盼等. NS-2 网络模拟基础与应用[M]. 北京：国防工业出版社,2008

[8] 任泰明. TCP/IP 协议与网络编程[M]. 西安：西安电子科技大学出版社,2004

[9] http://netcourse.xjtu.edu.cn/,西安交通大学计算机网络国家精品课程网站

[10] http://www.usstmba.cn/chenjq/www2/wl.asp,上海理工大学计算机网络精品课程网站

[11] 王忠民,王劲松,赵文祥等. 计算机专业英语[M]. 西安：西安电子科技大学出版社,2007

[12] 刘艺,王春生. 计算机英语[M]. 北京：机械工业出版社,2013

[13] Liu Y, Zhou G. Key technologies and applications of internet of things[C]Intelligent Computation Technology and Automation (ICICTA)，2012 Fifth International Conference on. IEEE，2012：197-200

[14] (美)Behrouz A. Forouzan，Sophia Chung Fegan. Data Communications and Networking (Fourth Edition)[M]. 吴时霖等译. 北京：机械工业出版社,2007

[15] (美)Behrouz A. Forouzan，Sophia Chung Fegan. Data Communications and Networking (Fifth Edition) [M]. 吴时霖等译. 北京：机械工业出版社,2013

[16] Atzori L, Iera A, Morabito G. *The internet of things：A survey*[J]. Computer Networks, 2010, 54 (15)：2787-2805

[17] Roman R, Najera P, Lopez J. *Securing the Internet of Things*[J]. Computer, 2011, 44(9)：51-58

[18] Armbrust M, Fox A, Griffith R, et al. *A view of cloud computing*[J]. Communications of the ACM, 2010, 53(4)：50-58

[19] Velte T, Velte A, Elsenpeter R. *Cloud computing, a practical approach* [M]. McGraw-Hill, Inc. , 2009

[20] Zhang Q, Cheng L, Boutaba R. *Cloud computing：state-of-the-art and research challenges*[J]. Journal of Internet Services and Applications, 2010, 1(1)：7-18

[21] Dikaiakos M D, Katsaros D, Mehra P, et al. *Cloud computing：Distributed Internet computing for IT and scientific research*[J]. Internet Computing, IEEE, 2009, 13(5)：10-13

[22] Kaufman C, Perlman R, Speciner M. *Network security：private communication in a public world* [M]. Prentice Hall Press, 2002

[23] Bishop M. *What is computer security?* [J]. Security & Privacy, IEEE, 2003, 1(1)：67-69

[24] Perrig A, Stankovic J, Wagner D. *Security in wireless sensor networks*[J]. Communications of the ACM, 2004, 47(6)：53-57